RACE AND SOCIETY

Titles in this series

THE DEFENCE
OF HUMAN RIGHTS
IN
LATIN AMERICA

(Sixteenth to eighteenth centuries)

Silvio Zavala

UNESCO

*Published in 1964 by the United Nations
Educational, Scientific and Cultural Organization
Place de Fontenoy, Paris-7ᵉ
Printed by Casterman, Tournai*

. . . That the great and terrible war which has now ended was a war made possible by the denial of the democratic principles of the dignity, equality and mutual respect of men, and by the propagation in their place, through ignorance and prejudice, of the doctrine of the inequality of men and races.

Preamble to the Constitution of Unesco
London, 16 November 1945

Dedicated to the memory of ALFRED MÉTRAUX

In this work, Mr. S. Zavala follows the thought of the Spanish jurists and theologians at grips with the problems set by the conquest, evangelizing and governing of the native peoples of the New World so alien in appearance, customs and dress to the conquistadors. It was by a slow progression that these thinkers—always keen of intellect and ever ready for disputation—came to recognize the natural rights of such peoples to live and be free, prerogatives which we understand today under the term 'human rights'.

It would be perhaps more exact to say that the ideological impact of the discovery of the New World was among the determining causes of the great leap forward which the notion of the unity of mankind was to take in the years that followed. The idea of unity of the world was imposed upon Western man and by its own internal logic it transformed the ancient expression . . . *humani nihil a me alienum puto* into . . . *nullum hominem a me alienum puto*, as said by Unamuno, himself a pure product of the end of the colonial age in the country of the conquistadors. Because of its history and the peculiarities of its modern settlement, America was a liberalizing factor and the efforts of these Spaniards and their desire for more justice and equity are not unlike the present-day struggle to put an end to the discrimination of all kinds which still weighs heavily upon human relationships.

American—or shall we say Americanist—thought has had a strong influence on international law and on the ideals of collaboration among peoples. Hence, the publication of Mr. S. Zavala's work, which accords well with the aims of Unesco, is a direct application of resolution 3.22 adopted by the General Conference at its sixth session in 1951 and authorizing the Director-General 'to undertake . . . a critical inventory of the methods and techniques employed for facilitating the social integration of groups which do not participate fully in the life of the national community by reason of their ethnical or cultural characteristics . . . .'

As with all the publications in this series, it is understood that the statements made and opinions expressed in this work are the author's own and do not necessarily reflect the views of Unesco.

CONTENTS

Contents

The discovery of the New World, naturally enough, was a matter that deeply stirred the consciences of men of letters and learning. In his *Historia de las Indias* Gómara wrote that the greatest event since the creation of the world, with the exception of the incarnation and death of Christ, was the discovery of that part of the earth.

The ideological consequences of Colombus's great venture manifested themselves in a variety of ways.

As regards geographical knowledge, men were to live thenceforward in a larger and fuller world. The voyage undertaken by Magellan and Elcan offers some indication as to the way the whole of Europe reacted to this extension of the field of human activity. And, as Antonio de Ulloa observed with some discernment in his *Relación Histórica del Viage a la América Meridional*, published in Madrid in 1748, not only had previously unknown countries been discovered, but these new discoveries served to bring about a clearer and better understanding of the Old World, since 'just as the New World owed its discovery to the Old, so it paid its debt by revealing to the latter its true lineaments, hitherto not fully realized or acknowledged'.

The natural sciences were enriched by the revelation of new botanical and zoological species, whence originated the interminable controversy —to be resumed in the eighteenth century—concerning their quality as compared with those of Europe.

The origin and nature of American man likewise attracted the attention of observers; but here speculation was not confined to the realm of anthropology—it also included religious and political elements.

For instance, the origin of man in America was explained in terms of Biblical traditions, although Acosta, in his *Historia Natural y Moral de las Indias*, showed a more scientific attitude by drawing attention to the northern route communicating with Asia.

The existence of species of human monsters was believed in long before Colombus's discovery. Pliny speaks of them in his *Historia Naturalis*. Later, St. Augustine, in his *De Civitate Dei*, records that such monsters appeared in pagan stories and in the mosaics adorning the public square in Carthage; and he expresses doubts whether they really belonged to the human race and, therefore, whether they were descended from Adam.

As early as 1622 a picture was published in Venice of a strange figure representing a supposed inhabitant of Brazil, which was none other than the 'dog man' of Pliny's *Historia*.

The exploration of America helped to prove the non-existence of any such fantastic beings; but Spain did not find an empty continent.

11

Consequently, her action was bound to be political, concerned as it was with other men in organized societies, whether wandering tribes, such as the Chichimecan, the Pampean, etc., or more advanced empires like those of the Aztecs or the Incas.

It is understandable, therefore, that the colonization of America gave rise to an abundant political literature in which discussion centred round the following problems: What are the grounds on which the dealings of Europeans with indigenous peoples can be justified? How ought recently discovered peoples to be governed?

At first sight, there would of course seem to be little ideological significance in a subject such as the conquest of America, which was largely the work of unlettered men, as in the notable case of Francisco Pizarro, the conqueror of Peru. Even when the soldiers knew how to read and write, or could depend on the advice of monks, men of letters or clerks, their undertakings were presumably prompted solely by the desire to serve, by force of arms, the ends of covetousness and exploitation, concealed behind the façade of a Christian crusade. This was the view adopted by many writers of the eighteenth and nineteenth centuries.

It is well to note, however, the existence of a particular line of thought with which the events of the Conquest are not unconnected. It is in terms of this that can be understood the campaign, initiated by ecclesiastics and enlightened officials, to bring the conduct of the *conquistadores* and colonizers into conformity with principles of greater justice. Moreover, the doctrine underlying the institutions designed to regulate the new Hispano-American society was not uninfluenced by the political philosophy which was the fruit of centuries of European culture. Hence the inevitable connexions with theology and morals—for in sixteenth-century Spain the tendency was to view human problems from the standpoint of conscience. This is brought out clearly in such works as the *Sumas de tratos y contratos*, where the theologian sets out to make the merchant aware of the dangers lying in wait for his soul. In the same way, political treatises dealt with the welfare of the conscience of rulers as well as of warriors—such as the *conquistadores*—exposed as they were to continual temptation.

It should be noted that the political theory to which we shall refer in this paper was concerned with the New World, while the ideological elements on which it was based came from Europe. Was it, then, an initial episode in the history of American ideas, or simply one more stage in European thought, related to events that had occurred overseas?

There is no denying that the main contribution in the realm of ideas was European; but, in opposition to the idea that America's role was purely passive, it should be borne in mind that recourse to European ideas for the purpose of interpreting the problems of the new continent had its counterpart in modifications—great or small—introduced, as a result of the new discovery, into the traditional culture of Europe.

Some of the thinkers who evolved the political philosophy of the Conquest had never been to the New World; others were '*indianos*', that is to say, Europeans with experience of life on the other side of the Atlantic. A certain, very understandable, difference may be observed between their respective lines of thought. Moreover, variations characteristic of the creole, the mestizo or the Indian soon arose in the attitude towards the New Continent.

In any case, the events of the Conquest contributed towards defining the problems of doctrine, towards giving them a practical content, while ideological activity, in turn, exerted an influence on historical development. This explains the close connexion between the political thought of that time and the institutions in America designed to regulate a society in which European settlers were living side by side with indigenous peoples. Thus we have a political philosophy in contact with the real problems of penetration and settlement in new lands.

It is clear that the various theories that were propounded concerning the first contact of the New World with Europe are not merely of historical interest, but have their significance for modern times; for the circumstances attendant upon the expansion of powerful nations and the government of colonial peoples have arisen on more than one occasion. Thus we may regard the Spanish Conquest of America as a useful intimation of what we are now experiencing in international and political life, although neither the terminology nor the individual historical circumstances are identical.

It will be noted that the first of the following studies is concerned with the contact between Christians and infidels. This is a mediaeval type of approach to the problem, but one which still had current significance at the time of the discovery of America.

However, it was not the only ideological trend to have had a perceptible influence upon speculation concerning the Conquest. Some Scholastic thinkers and others trained in Renaissance ways of thought adopted the classical theory of the relationship of civilized men to barbarians, proclaiming the natural subservience of the Indians and the right of the Spaniards to subdue them by force.

In contrast to this theory came the ideology of Stoic and Christian origin which affirmed the freedom of the indigenous peoples and viewed the mission of the colonizers as a civilizing guardianship. It was this which finally prevailed in the ideological and legislative relationship between Spain and Indo-America.

In a later chapter I shall mention some of the contributions of eighteenth-century thought to the controversy between the partisans of servitude and those of freedom, considering more especially, of course, those aspects which relate to America.

These, in outline, are the ideas of which I propose to trace the development. I shall dispense with erudite references here, but readers who are interested in having fuller details may refer to the short bibliography given at the end of this work.

My study *La filosofía política en la conquista de América*, published by the Fondo de Cultura Económica, Mexico, in 1947, has served as a basis for the present summary, which has been produced with the consent of the publishers.

As is well known, there is an abun-
dance of documentary material concerning the Spanish conquest of
America, including religious and
administrative documents, and others
written by private individuals, all

of unquestionable value as a means of understanding the spirit of the
colonizing process.

If we consider the expressions used in these documents, we see that
the national interest, which predominates in more modern undertakings,
did not in those days preclude the custom inherited from the Middle
Ages of viewing the problem in the light of the progress of Christianity
at the cost of the pagan or infidel peoples.

This view of the political problem of the conquest of Indo-America
finds its explanation in the historical panorama of the times leading up
to the discovery.

A map of the Christian and Moslem worlds in about the year 1000
—such as the map published by Menéndez Pidal—shows Christianity
surrounded by Islam, with an extensive area of penetration on the
western flank representing the invasion of the Iberian peninsula. Later,
in the fifteenth century, the fall of Constantinople clearly imperilled
the eastern frontier of the Christian world. But the Spanish reconquest
pushed back the old threat from the West, and at the same time opened
the door to European expansion along the coasts of Africa and in the
Canary Islands, Asia and America.

This advance was accompanied by a corresponding shift in the ideas
concerning Christians and infidels, like an echo of the struggle that had
been waged in Europe throughout so many centuries.

Spain was a country profoundly affected by the political rivalry
between the Christian and Saracen worlds. Already in the eleventh
century the struggle was marked by religious intransigence.

A reflection of this attitude may be noted in the *Leyes de Partidas*,
which lists among the just causes of war: 'the first, in order that the
peoples shall increase their faith and that those who would combat it
shall be destroyed....'

The spirit of this thirteenth-century pronouncement appears again
unchanged in a document issued by Ferdinand and Isabella in 1479:
'We are sending certain of our captains and followers to the conquest
of the Gran Canaria, against the infidel Canary islanders, enemies of our
Holy Catholic faith, who are in the island and whom it is urgent to
capture.'

In the New World, at the end of the second decade of the sixteenth
century, Hernán Cortés declared that he was 'fighting for the Faith'.
And he assured the soldiers who followed him in the final phase of the

conquest of Mexico, that they had just causes and reasons on their side: 'one being to fight for the spreading of our faith and to combat barbarians. . . .'

Bernal Díaz del Castillo, in his *Historia Verdadera de la Conquista de la Nueva España*, speaks of the good services rendered by the *conquistadores* 'to God, to His Majesty and to all Christianity'.

In court and literary circles in Spain it is easy to find precedents for and parallels to the thought expressed by these men-at-arms. We need only recall the negotiation of the Bulls relating to the cession of sovereignty and evangelization in Indo-America issued by Pope Alexander VI, and the appreciation shown by the Crown for action concerning the propagation of the Faith.

The chronicler Gómara, conscious of the variety of motives underlying the Conquest, puts this speech with subtle irony into the mouth of Cortés: 'The main reason for our coming to these parts is to extol and preach the faith of Christ, although at the same time honour and profit, which can seldom be contained in one sack, follow in our path.'

Despite the intensity and the peculiarities of the Iberian crusade, we must not think that these tendencies were exclusive to the people of the Peninsula. It is, indeed, possible to discover a general doctrine held by European thinkers in regard to the relation of Christianity to the infidel peoples.

Already in the thirteenth century, we find some ideas which are of interest in this connexion.

The canonist Enrico da Susa, better known as 'the Ostian' (d. 1271), believed the Pope to be the Universal Vicar of Jesus Christ and, consequently, to have authority not only over Christians but also over all infidels, since the powers which Christ received from the Father were plenary. And it seemed to him that, since the coming of the Redeemer, all primacy, dominion and jurisdiction had been taken away from the infidels and transferred to the faithful, by right and with just reason, by him who held the supreme power and was infallible.

According to this doctrine, the entitlement to their kingdoms which infidels might have had by virtue of natural law and the law of nations before the advent of Christ, disappeared as a result of that event, temporal power reverting to the Pontiff of Rome, who might, if he deemed fit, claim authority over infidels. In the meantime, the latter enjoyed only a precarious tenancy of their kingdoms in the form of concessions from the Holy See in Rome.

Although it had no ideological connexion with the doctrine of 'the Ostian', but as an example of another position that weakened the right of the infidel in the face of the Christian advance, the theory of John Wycliffe (1324-84) may be recalled: all human law presupposes as its cause divine law; consequently, every dominion that is just according to men, presupposes a dominion that is just according to God. As the unjust man or the man in mortal sin is without grace, he does not properly hold dominion.

It is true that the Council of Constance (1415-16) condemned this doctrine; but it is not without interest to note that Francisco de Vitoria thought it necessary to contest it again in dealing with the just entitlements to Indo-America, maintaining, logically, that partisans of the doctrine could affirm that the barbarians of the New World held no dominion, because they were still in a state of mortal sin.

In contrast to these attitudes it is possible to find, in European thought from the thirteenth to sixteenth centuries, other more generous attitudes concerning the relations between Christianity and the infidel peoples.

Innocent IV (d. 1254) admitted that infidels might lawfully hold dominion and possessions and exercise jurisdiction, since these were not made solely for the faithful but for every rational creature. Consequently, it was not lawful for the Pope or the faithful to take from infidels the goods and the jurisdiction which they held without sin. But Christ, and consequently the Pope, had authority over all men in law though not in fact. Accordingly, the Roman See might punish infidels who acted against the law of nature: for instance sodomites and idolaters.

As this theory acknowledged that the basis of dominion was simply the rational power of man and not his religious state, it gave scope for greater tolerance concerning the rights of infidels.

In the same line of thought, in the *Summa Theologica* of Thomas Aquinas (1225-74), it is held that dominion and preference are introduced by virtue of human law; on the other hand, the distinction between the faithful and infidels is a matter of divine law. But the latter, which emanates from grace, does not annul human law, which is based on natural reason. Consequently, the distinction between faithful and infidel, considered in itself, does not abolish even the dominion which infidels may hold over Christians. It is true that St. Thomas later modified the doctrine, admitting that the superiority of the infidels might justly be abolished by a judgement or order of the Church, which exercised the authority of God; because the infidels, on account of their unbelief, deserved to lose their authority over the faithful, who were to become the sons of God. But, as the foregoing suggests, it is not a question of an all-prevailing right on the part of Christianity as against the complete helplessness of the unbelievers; it is rather that, on reflexion, Christian thought finds within itself those elements of Natural Law and Reason which are the heritage of all mankind.

The ideology of the Hispano-American Conquest shows the influence of the general doctrines indicated above, and may be divided into two stages.

At the beginning, the Spanish monarchs wanted to know what were the just rights entitling them to dominion over Indo-America and how they should govern the recently discovered peoples. They consulted their theologians and men of letters, and one of the most distinguished jurists of the Court, Doctor Juan López de Palacios Rubios, wrote a treatise on these questions in about 1514. Las Casas attacked him severely because he considered that Palacios Rubios had allowed himself to be influenced by the 'errors' of 'the Ostian'. In fact, Ferdinand the Catholic's adviser maintained that Christ was sovereign in the spiritual and temporal sense and delegated these powers to the Pope and that therefore infidel kingdoms had no independence in relation to the Roman See and were obliged to submit to its authority if so required. Like the thirteenth-century canonist, he considered that possession as far as the infidels were concerned was only in the nature of a temporary tenancy until such time as Rome claimed her right.

Palacios Rubios also drew up an 'injunction' *(requerimiento)* which the *conquistadores* were to read to the Indians in the New World. It began by summarily explaining the Christian doctrine, so that the infidels might know who Christ was, who the Pope was, and what right the Christians had to require them to submit to their authority. The last paragraph revealed the coercive nature of this statement. When the Indians had been told that all men were neighbours and descendants of Adam, they were to be asked to acknowledge the Church and the Pope, and the King and Queen as holding authority over these lands by Papal delegation. If they were willing to submit, they would be received in all love and charity, and their wives and children and lands would be left free to them, and they would not be compelled to become Christians, unless on being informed of the truth they should desire to be converted, in which case the king would grant them many favours. If they refused to obey, the captain, with the help of God, would make war on them, and capture them and their wives and children, and make them slaves and sell them as such.

As the text specifies, the infidels were not to be compelled to become Christians, for conversion was to be voluntary; but they were to be required to submit to the authority of Rome, as delegated to the Spaniards, it being considered that in this case the Church possessed authority of a temporal order. The consequences ensuing upon refusal by the Indians were a part of the contemporary conception of just war, slavery being a result of it. What the writer endeavours to do is to justify the reason for warlike action. As we have already seen, in the last resort everything depends on the scope accorded to the right of jurisdiction of Christianity over the infidel world.

The above-mentioned 'injunction' was used in the conquests of Darien, Mexico, Nueva Galicia, Peru, etc.

Difficulties arose in practice, due partly to the natural failure of the ndians to understand, on account of the difference between their anguage and civilization and those of Europe, and partly to the unscru-ulousness of the soldiers responsible for applying the clauses of the omplicated text.

In certain chronicles of the time (for instance, that of Enciso, rinted in 1519), it is related that certain Indian chiefs or *caciques*, f Castilla del Oro were enjoined in the manner described above and eplied that, as regards what was said to them about there being only ne God, who ruled heaven and earth, that was as it should be; but that he Pope was giving away what was not his, and that the king who sked for it and took it must be a madman, for he was demanding what elonged to others; and that the captain should go and capture him and hey would impale his head upon a post, as had been done with other nemies of theirs, which they showed him.

As a result of that reply, the *conquistador* took the country by force.

In another case, the chronicler Fernández de Oviedo relates that the overnor Pedrarias Dávila gave him the *requerimiento*, as if intending that e should read it to the Indians, or as if assuming that there would be omeone present who could make them understand it and that they vould be willing to listen; but, when shown the paper, they took little otice. In the presence of all the soldiers, Oviedo said to Pedrarias: Sir, it seems to me that these Indians do not want to listen to the heological content of this statement, and that you do not have anyone to xplain it to them. Pray keep it, if you will, until we have some of these Indians in gaol where they can take it in slowly, and the Lord Bishop an make them understand.' And he handed back the document in the nidst of general laughter.

The practical difficulties were accompanied by an extensive revision f the theories, especially by Spanish writers, although there were some mportant contributions by thinkers from other parts of Europe.

One relevant text was written by a professor in Paris, a Scotsman named John Major, who, in his Commentary on Book II of the Sentences, published in 1510, maintained that the kingdom of Christ was not of this world and that the Pope was the Vicar of Christ solely in spiritual matters; nor was the Emperor lord of all the earth.

At that time the Spanish monarch did not yet hold the title of Emperor. Moreover, when Charles I succeeded in adopting it, Indo-America did not on that account cease to belong directly to the crown of Castille and León. Consequently, the theory of Papal authority, linked through Pope Alexander's Bulls to Spanish sovereignty over the New World, had more influence in the altercation concerning America than the idea of the Empire, although this was brought in as a supporting argument because it implied claims to universality.

In addition to his insistence on the revision of those absolute European powers which might aspire to give an appearance of legitimacy to the governance of Indo-America, Major stood firmly by the generous principle we have already noted in Innocent IV and St. Thomas, to the effect that dominion is not based either on faith or on charity, but on natural law, in virtue of which the infidel may have freedom, property and jurisdiction.

Furthermore, as the European world widened its geographical and human experience, it began to see more clearly the differences between various types of infidels in regard both to religion and to the degree of hostility manifested towards Christians, and therefore to realize that the behaviour of Christians towards them need not be uniform.

Major, for instance, pointed out that there were different categories of infidels: those who had taken possession of lands belonging to Christians, such as the Turks who ruled over Greece; others who had obtained their lands not by seizure but in accordance with just right for non-Christians. The fate of those in the second category depended upon their assent, or opposition, to the preaching of the faith by Christians. According to Major, the temporal power of Christians over infidels could be justified either as a means preparatory to the propagation of the Faith or as a posterior measure for the conservation of faith already accepted by non-Christians.

In this doctrine the idea of the predominance of the Christian over the infidel is not completely absent. The religious aim of converting the heathen becomes the real justification for the expansion of European jurisdictional powers. Major also accepted the classic justification of imperialism, based on the differences of reason as between men; but we shall consider that point later.

Another thinker who is of the greatest importance, both as regards the subject itself and on account of his influence on the Spanish school, is Cardinal Cayetano, Tomás de Vío (1469-1534). In his commentaries on St. Thomas, printed in 1517, he made a distinction between various categories of infidels: those who, in fact and in law, were the subjects of Christian princes—for instance, Jews living in Christian lands; other infidels who were the subjects of Christians in law but not in fact, such as those occupying lands belonging to Christians (as in the Holy Land); and, lastly, infidels who were not the subjects of Christian princes either in law or in fact, namely, pagans who had never been subjects of the Roman Empire, inhabitants of lands where the name 'Christian' had never been heard of (this is the part applicable to the Indians in the New World). These infidels were not deprived of their property because of their unbelief, for property was a matter of positive law and unbelief a matter of divine law, which did not annul positive law. Neither a king nor an emperor, nor the Roman Church was entitled to wage war against

hem in order to occupy their lands or to place them under temporal
ubjection, because there was no cause for a just war.

This shows that the infidel world was no longer regarded as an enemy
n the mass, indiscriminately denoted by the hostile term 'Saracen'.
During the conquest of the Canary Islands differences between the
Guanches and the Moors were observed, which produced certain doctrinal
listinctions. And, in matters relating to the New World, from that time
onwards the obvious differences between the Indians and the
Mohammedans were given full theoretical recognition.

Cayetano's writings contain other notable observations concerning
he method of penetration that could be used in America. He thought
hat this method should be apostolic, that it should consist in convincing
he heathen and not in acts of violence. For Christ, to whom all power
vas given in heaven and earth, did not send soldiers to take possession
•f the world; He sent saintly preachers like sheep among wolves;
Christians would sin gravely if they sought to spread the Christian faith
•y force of arms; they would not be lawful lords over the Indians but
vould be committing grand larceny and would be obliged to restitute
vhat they had taken, like assailants and unjust owners. Preachers, good
nen, should be sent to these infidels, men who would convert them to
God by word and example, and not men who would oppress and scan-
lalize them and make them twofold sons of the devil in the fashion of
he Pharisees.

Among the Spanish authors, we find Las Casas, better known for his
ampaigns in defence of the Indians than for his theories, stating that
mong the infidels who had never heard of Christ or received the faith,
here were real nobles, kings and princes, and they were entitled to
heir nobility, dignity and royal pre-eminence by natural law and the
aw of nations. Obviously alluding to 'the Ostian's' doctrine, in order to
hallenge it through his disciple Palacios Rubios, he denied that with
he advent of Christ infidels had lost, either collectively or individually,
ny position of authority. To believe the contrary was wicked. In his
iew, the jurisdiction of the indigenous chiefs should be brought into
onformity with Spanish sovereignty, the latter fulfilling the function
•f a 'quasi-empire'. The use of arms to help forward the evangelization
•f the Indians—admitted by Ginés de Sepúlveda, among others—induced
im to compare this conquest with those of the followers of Mohammed
nd so to pave the way for the Mexican friar Servando de Mier who,
vriting during the independence period, was to call the Spanish
onquistadores of the sixteenth century 'apostles of the scimitar'.

Francisco de Vitoria developed these ideas to the full. He rejected
s unlawful the right of the Pope and the Emperor to universal temporal
lominion. Following the Thomist tradition, he stated that the rights
•f political organizations and of dominion over property were based

on natural reason and human—not divine—law and, therefore, were compatible with the distinction between Christians and unbelievers. To those who considered the condition of infidelity as a ground for loss of the right to dominion, he replied: 'The condition of infidelity is not a bar either to natural law or to human law; but dominion is a matter either of natural law or of positive law; therefore absence of the Faith is not a bar to it.' Again, in answer to those who invoked the question of mortal sins, he replied as follows: 'Dominion is founded on the image of God; but man is in the image of God by virtue of his nature, that is to say, by his reasoning powers, which are not lost as the result of mortal sin. Hence, since the image of God, its basis, is not lost by mortal sin, neither is dominion.' It is therefore understandable that Vitoria should conclude that part of his dissertation with these words: 'Before the coming of the Spaniards to America, the barbarians were the true owners, both public and private'.

The lawful grounds he admitted were: natural communication between peoples, which did not necessarily involve political domination; propagation of the faith, which could be peaceable and leave the possession of the infidels unharmed, if they did not resist it; preservation of the Faith, once accepted; safeguards against tyranny on the part of the natives, 'whether by superiors over their subjects, or through laws oppressing the innocent, such as those ordering human sacrifices' real and voluntary choice, that is, 'if the barbarians—both the chief and the others—conscious of the intelligent and wise administration and the humanity of the Spaniards, should spontaneously wish to receive the King of Spain as their Ruler'; alliances, such as those between the soldiers of Hernán Cortés and the Tlascaltecs to attack the Mexicans; and, without going so far as to affirm it fully, the predominance of the civilized man over the barbarian, approved by Aristotle.

Precedents of this kind explain how Father Espinosa, in a book entitled *Origen y Milagros de Nuestra Señora de Candalaria*, printed in Seville in 1594, drawing a parallel between the case of the Canary Islanders and that of the American Indians, was able to affirm: 'It is a certainty, according to divine and human law, that the war waged by the Spaniards, both against the natives of these islands (the Canary Islands) and against the Indians in the West, was unjust and without good reason, for neither did they possess lands belonging to Christians nor did they go out beyond their own boundaries in order to infest or molest other lands. And if it be said that the Spaniards brought them the Gospel, then it should have been with preaching and admonition and not with drum and flag, entreating and not compelling, but that subject has already been discussed elsewhere.'

So we reach a stage where Europeans had revised the theory favourable to the power of the Pope in temporal matters and had limited the universal jurisdiction of the Emperor; and, in addition, they had strengthened the rights of the infidels to their freedom, possessions and kingdoms. In these circumstances, the grounds which could justify the relationship of Christians to unbelievers had to be fairer and more universal. Faced with the advance of Christianity, the non-Christian world did not find itself deprived of fundamental human rights.

The controversy on the Spanish-American problem incidentally helped to clarify the thorny question of the relationship between spiritual and temporal power, which had aroused so much feeling in Europe. In fact, Spain rose up in defence of Catholicism after the Reformation; but, generally speaking, her thinkers did not follow the criteria of the Ostian', but agreed with Vitoria that the Pope's power was spiritual and that it was only for spiritual ends that he possessed temporal powers. This attitude had precedents, as can be seen in the case of Torquemada, and found expression in the ideas of Belarmino, who quoted Vitoria with veneration.

The progress in political doctrine concerning the conquest of Indo-America was reflected in institutional changes, ranging from the abandonment of the 'injunction' to the establishment of the ordinances of Philip II in 1573. In these ordinances the term 'conquest' was replaced by 'pacification', 'for, as the discoveries are to be made with as much peace and charity as we would desire, we do not wish that their designation should give occasion or pretext for the doing of violence or injury to the Indians'. But the Crown did not abandon the system of private financing which served as a basis for the organization of ventures for discovery and colonization, in the absence of financial support from the public authorities. This system was held largely responsible for the uncontrollable desire of the soldiers to compensate themselves for their costs and effort at the expense of the Indians.

Some time later, in Law 9, Section 4, Book III, of the *Recopilación de las Leyes de Indias*, published in 1680 and drawn up, in more definite terms, on the basis of previously existing provisions, the following order is to be found: 'that war may not, and shall not, be waged against the Indians in any province for the purpose of making them adopt the Holy Catholic Faith or give obedience to us, or for any other reason'.

In other words, war came to be forbidden by law as an instrument of religious and political penetration in the New World. A strange but understandable corollary of the conquests made since the end of the fifteenth century.

As regards the prerogatives of the indigenous population, the legislator, applying the theories of natural law explained above, came to admit both their personal freedom and their property. In the political sphere —and here the self-interest of the royal administration played its part— the offices of the tribal chiefs *(cacicazgos)* were retained, though not

23

with the wide range of functions for which Las Casas had asked. General directions were given for the customs of the Indians to be respected, when these were not contrary to the Christian faith or to good order.

These institutional aims were opposed to the requirements and to the cupidity of the group who exercised control over the actual processes of colonization. A conflict arose between law and fact: between written law, on the one hand, and practice in the provinces, on the other. The Indian might be free as far as theory and law in Spain were concerned, but the exercise of this freedom in practice might be hampered by powerful obstacles of a social nature. Nevertheless, the ideas of freedom and protection of the indigenous peoples formed an inseparable part of this complex historical scene, as attributes of the Spanish conscience in America. The conquerors themselves came to revise their early attitude of domination and violence, and adopted a more liberal one than that accepted at the end of the Middle Ages in relations with non-Christian peoples.

As we have seen, the advance of
Christianity against the unbelievers
was an essential factor in thought
relating to the conquest of America;
but if we examine the terminology of
the sixteenth century we find other

expressions which bear witness to the presence of concepts of a more
definitely political nature, though not without a religious or moral tinge.

I refer to the envisaging of the Conquest as the domination of barbarians by civilized men; in other words, to the consideration of the
problem from the point of view of reason. In this case we must not
look for precedents in the development of theological and canonical
thought in Europe from the thirteenth to the sixteenth centuries, but
in the political philosophy of the Greeks.

Aristotle, in the part of his *Politics* devoted to the study of slavery,
puts the question whether this institution is natural. He recalls that
certain authors consider it against nature for one man to be the servant
of another, for the distinction between free man and slave is a con-
ventional one and there is no natural difference between men;
consequently the relationship is an unjust one, based on force.

But, although Aristotle takes account of the writers who hold that
opinion, he for his part accepts the idea that slavery is natural and that
its philosophical basis is to be found in the differences existing between
men as regards the use of reason.

He asserts that those whose function is based on the use of the body,
and from whom no more than that can be obtained, are slaves by nature;
that is to say, men who, 'in so far as they come in contact with reason,
may be able to perceive it, but do not possess it in themselves'.

It is not necessary to go into the details of Aristotle's thought on this
point, but two important aspects of it should be emphasized. In the
first place, this hierarchy of reason in which servitude has its place
is related to a general order in nature, which involves subjection of
the imperfect to the more perfect. This principle explains the predominance of the soul over the body, for instance, or of man over woman.
The same must necessarily occur among all men. The wise, or those
fully possessed of reason, must have dominion over the unskilled or
barbarians who do not attain to it in the same degree. For the latter,
servitude is a just and appropriate institution. The other aspect is the
admission by Aristotle of the use of force for establishing the dominion
of civilized peoples over barbarians. War, he asserts, is just when waged
against men who, though intended by nature to be governed, will not
submit.

This doctrine is usually interpreted as a manifestation of the Hellenic
sense of superiority over barbarian peoples. But we should not forget

that other cosmopolitan and equalitarian ideas, not in conformity with that attitude, had begun to develop in the classical world.

These various ideas and doctrines of the Ancient World penetrated to Imperial Rome. Conquests and slavery spread in proportion as the Romans extended their power over foreign peoples. But in Seneca we find the statement that, though the body may be in slavery, the soul is free. This idea made it possible to redeem the dignity of man even in the most wretched social condition.

The early Fathers of the Church took over this ideological legacy and amended it. In the state of innocence there was no servitude; all men were said to be born free. It was not God's will that man should exercise dominion over man; but the fall through sin had opened the way to slavery, as to other institutions in the law of nations which were likened to bitter but necessary medicine. However, equality and freedom of origin were in a sense indestructible and inalienable; even in the state of the world at the time, though the body might be in subjection, the mind and soul were free. The slave was capable of reason and virtue; he could even be superior to the man he served. And in man's relationship with God all differences of status were unimportant. All men, whether free or slaves, were called to a common life in Christ and in God, to acknowledge Him as their common Father and to consider each other as brothers.

So began the strange relationship between Christianity and slavery. Christ's doctrine was not of this world and, therefore, did not demand the abolition of servitude; but, as a consequence of its spiritual principles, it did not fail to have an influence on earthly institutions, in favour of freedom.

We cannot follow all the ramifications of these ideas through the Middle Ages and the Renaissance. It should, however, be borne in mind that Scholasticism gleaned from the works of St. Thomas Aquinas the heritage of Aristotelian thought, and that this was studied again with special interest by some Renaissance writers.

Both of the above trends of thought were to exert an influence on Spanish authors of treatises who concerned themselves with problems relating to the Conquest and the servitude of the Indians in the New World.

Perhaps the mediaeval text which contributed most to preserving and spreading the idea of natural servitude was the *De Regimine Principum*, attributed to St. Thomas Aquinas. It is now known that, from Chapter IV of Book II, it was probably written by Tolomeo of Lucca (d. 1326 or 1327). But writers in the thirteenth to the sixteenth centuries were not aware of this, and the authority, great in itself, which Aristotle enjoyed among them was strengthened by the supposed approval of the Angelic Doctor.

The *De Regimine Principum* recalls that Tolomeo in his *Quadripartito* proves that men's customs differ according to the differences in the constellations, on account of the influence of the stars on the power of the will.

This cosmographical explanation goes so far as to link up with the idea of servitude: every country is subject to celestial influences and that is why some countries are found to be suited to servitude and others to freedom.

Under cover of Aristotle's doctrine, the author of the *De Regimine Principum* maintained that among men there were some who were serfs by nature; lacking in reason because of some natural defect, they were better confined to servile work, since they could not make use of reason; and so their condition was said to be naturally just.

In fact, to judge by authentic texts such as the *Summa Theologica*, St. Thomas thought that, considered in the absolute, for a man to be a serf was not in accordance with natural reason except in relation to the utility to be derived therefrom, inasmuch as it was useful for the serf to be governed by the wiser man and for the latter to be served by the former. Servitude in the law of nations was natural, not according to absolute reason, but in this latter more restricted sense, i.e. on account of its useful consequences.

The Scotsman John Major, a Nominalist professor in Paris, of whom mention was made earlier in connexion with the subject of Christians and infidels, seems to have been the first Scholastic writer to apply the Aristotelian concept of natural servitude to the problem of government raised by Columbus' discovery.

In his work published in 1510, he accepts the geographical explanation regarding the origin of the barbarian state, though not in the general terms to be found in the *De Regimine Principum* but with reference to the Indians in the New World: 'These people live like beasts. Tolomeo in his *Quadripartito* related that on either side of the Equator, and under the Poles, there lived savage men; and that is precisely what experience has confirmed.' Major then goes on to link this statement with the classic argument concerning servitude: 'Therefore the first one to occupy those lands may in law rule over their inhabitants, for it is clear that they are by nature serfs'. He invokes the authority of the Philosopher in the *Politics* and recalls the passage referring to a statement by the poets that the Greeks ruled over the barbarians because the latter were by nature wild and savage.

There was nothing new either in this geographical explanation of the condition of the barbarian or in the doctrine of natural servitude. Indeed, Major did not conceal his sources of inspiration. But what was original in his work was that he extended these ideas to the case of the American Indians.

At about this time, the Spanish Crown had called the famous Council of Burgos (1512), at which theologians and jurists argued concerning the conquest and government of Indo-America.

On that occasion Palacios Rubios wrote a treatise which we have already considered in another connexion but to which we must now refer again because of what it has to say on the question of servitude. It distinguishes clearly between two kinds of servitude: legal and natural. Concerning the first, the author states that at the beginning of the world men were born free and legitimate, and that slavery was unknown. The Scriptures confirm this assertion: God created man to have dominion over the fowls of the air, the fish of the sea and the beasts of the earth; for it was His will that rational man, made in His image, should have dominion only over the non-rational and not over other men. In a sense, nature created all men free and equal. In the beginning, therefore, when nature alone governed man, and before there were any written laws, there was no difference between the natural child and the legitimate child, for in olden times children were legitimate by the very fact of their birth and nature made all children free, as being of free parents. It was wars that first gave rise to slavery.

But we must not think that Palacios Rubios was attacking the institution of servitude as accepted by the society of his times. He was merely formulating a doctrine on the origin of slavery: free and equalitarian status was not an inherent characteristic of a world that had fallen into sin, but only of the primary state of innocence. God granted freedom to the human race, but wars, the separation of peoples, the foundation of kingdoms and the distinction between dominions were introduced by the law of nations. This law proclaimed that what had been captured in war could become the property of those who had captured it, and that, as the prize of victory, the vanquished should be slaves of the victor, in order to incite men to defend their country and to keep the vanquished alive instead of killing them. By virtue of this law, slavery encroached upon freedom; and men, who had previously been designated by one common name, now under the law of nations began to be of three classes—free men, slaves and freed-men.

As regards natural servitude, he explained—on the basis of Aristotle's *Politics*, the *De Regimine Principum* attributed to St.Thomas, and the work of the same title by Egidio Romano—that ruling and serving were necessary and useful functions. Nature provided what was required in this respect. Some men were so superior to others in intelligence and capacity that they seemed to be born expressly to command and dominate, whilst others were so uncouth and obtuse by nature that they seemed destined to obey and serve. From the moment when they were begotten, some were masters and others slaves.

We have already noted in connexion with the 'Injunction', the view held by Palacios Rubios that infidels who were reluctant to submit to Christian dominion, or to accept preachers of the Faith, gave cause for a just war and could be enslaved as a consequence thereof. Slavery in such circumstances was legal. But this writer also believed that, even if the infidels did not resist and if they accepted the ministers of the Faith, nevertheless, as some of them were so uncouth and incapable that they were absolutely unable to govern themselves, they could—in the broad sense—be called slaves, being born to serve and not to command, as Aristotle had maintained; and, like the ignorant creatures they were, it was for them to serve those who were wise, as a subject served his lord.

In other words, against the infidel who resisted one had recourse to war and legal slavery; against those who obeyed one might make use of natural servitude on the grounds of their unfitness or their barbarian state.

Now Palacios Rubios had already said that the second category could be called slaves 'in the broad sense'; he tells us tat the two types of infidelh are not subjected to the same kind of government. He explains, indeed, that the second type 'are, nevertheless, free and freeborn. . . . They are called serfs, that is to say, servants; and this kind of servitude, taken in the broad sense, was introduced under the law of nations, as it is appropriate for the unskilled man to be governed by the wise and experienced. According to this reasoning, and on grounds of utility, this form of slavery could be said to have been introduced by natural law.' Palacios Rubios invoked the authority of John Major in support of this point of view.

In Indo-America, the natural servitude referred to by Palacios Rubios, as distinct from strict or legal servitude, was presumably represented in practice by the institution of the *encomiendas* (estates with their Indian inhabitants, granted to colonizers by the Spanish Crown). The Indian subjected to this régime came to be regarded as a free man, though subject to a servitude 'in the broad sense'.

Writing about the same time, Friar Bernardo de Mesa of the Order of Preachers, after rejecting the arguments usually advanced with regard to the Indian question, accepted as the sole reason for natural servitude on the part of the Indians their lack of understanding and competence, and their inability to persevere in the Faith and in good behaviour. He accorded great importance to the geographical explanation, of which we have already seen some instances: the Indians were serfs perhaps, on account of the nature of the land; for there were some lands which the aspect of the heavens made subservient and which could not be governed unless some form of serfdom obtained there —as in France, Normandy and part of Dauphiné, where the inhabitants had always been ruled much like serfs. Friar Bernardo did not fail to take account, among the geographical circumstances, of the island situation of the Indians in the Antilles: their nature did not enable them to persevere in virtue, either because they were islanders and so by nature less constant—since the waters that surrounded them were controlled by the moon—or because of evil habits which always incline men to such ways.

This doctrine, so unflattering to islanders in general, met with frank opposition from other writers, including Las Casas, who stated: 'It would be well to ask this Friar and, had I known that he had expressed this opinion, I would have asked him, when I later made his acquaintance, if he realized what the result would have been if the islanders of England, Sicily, Crete, or those nearer to Spain, from the Balearic Islands, from Majorca, had been shared out amongst other peoples, simply because the moon controls the waters; or, again, if the people of Normandy and part of Dauphiné had been divided up here and there like flocks of cattle, for the purpose of preaching the Faith to them, keeping them in good order and bestowing other virtues upon them.'

This episode shows the extent to which the scientific beliefs of a period are apt to influence its political ideas.

Finally, Friar Bernardo de Mesa adopted the theory of a form of government compromising between freedom and slavery: the Indians could not be called serfs, although for their own good they had to be placed under some form of servitude (but not to such an extent that they could be considered as slaves), nor should they be given so much freedom as would be harmful to them.

It is clear that the problem had two aspects: the claims which the Spaniards could invoke to justify domination of the Indians, and the form of government under which these should be placed during the process of colonization. The populations more particularly concerned were the Indians of the Antilles and of the known shores of Central and South America. In the years before 1519 the principal civilizations of the continent of America had not yet been subjugated.

Let us now leave the Scholastic writers and consider the chief Spanish exponent of the doctrine of natural servitude: Ginés de Sepúlveda. He was not just another representative of Scholasticism but a man moulded by the Renaissance, who had frequented the Aristotelian circle of Pomponazzi in Italy. He read the Philosopher in the original and made an elegant Latin translation of the *Politics*. His own work, the *Democrates alter*, is a dialogue on the war against the Indians and appeared in 1547 when the peoples of central Mexico, Yucatan and Peru were already known; but the sight of these more advanced indigenous civilizations did nothing to temper the disdain he felt for the barbarian condition of the Indians. As a faithful disciple of classical thought, he deals with the question of the relations of the Spaniards with the Indians in a manner reminiscent of the attitude generally adopted by the Greeks towards the barbarians.

The two interlocutors in the dialogue are Democrates, the spokesman of the author, and Leopoldo, a German somewhat influenced by Lutheranism, whose part is to present the objections and difficulties.

Without beating about the bush, Democrates begins with the following assertion: 'Oh Leopoldo, if you know anything of the customs and the nature on either side, you will readily understand that the Spaniards have a perfect right to rule over these barbarians in the New World and the adjoining islands, for in wisdom, skill, virtue and humanity these people are as inferior to the Spaniards as children are to adults and women to men; there is as great a difference between them as there is between savagery and forbearance, between violence and moderation, almost—I am inclined to say—between monkeys and men.'

Sepúlveda had read the whole of the *Politics*, and he recalled the passage stating that if no other way were possible, it was fair to subdue by force of arms peoples who, on account of their natural condition, ought to obey others but refused to submit to their rule. As the greatest philosophers had affirmed, such a war would be just and in accordance with the law of nature.

Consequently, the difference noted by Sepúlveda between the reason possessed by Spaniards and by Indians sufficed to justify the domination of the latter by the former, through recourse to arms if need be.

Among the causes that gave rise to herile rule (or rule by a master) which was suited to certain nations, Sepúlveda admitted the following: being a serf by nature, due to having been born in certain climates and parts of the world; depravity of customs or some other reason which made it impossible to keep men in the path of duty. In his opinion, both these causes were relevant to the case of the Indians.

But further on, without giving undue importance to the geographical reason for servitude, which by its nature seemed to imply a certain physical immutability, Sepúlveda proclaimed the civilizing influence of Spanish rule over the barbarians. Not only, indeed, did wise men make use of these barbarians, but they raised them to a higher level of reason and a better way of life, in soar as their condition allowed of such improvement. So the writer compares Spain with Rome, and adds: 'What better or more salutary thing could happen to these barbarians than that they should come under the rule of a people whose wisdom, virtue and religion were to change them from barbarians—scarcely worthy to be called human beings—into civilized men, in so far as they were capable thereof; from being stupid and lustful to being upright and honest; from being wicked servants of the devils to being Christians and worshippers of the true God? They are now beginning to accept the Christian faith, thanks to the providence and diligence of the Emperor

Charles, that excellent and religious prince; they have already been given public preceptors in the humanities and the sciences, and—what is more important—teachers of religion and behaviour. For many and weighty reasons, therefore, these barbarians are under obligation by the law of nature to accept the Spaniards' rule, and this will be more profitable to them than to the Spaniards, for virtue, humanity and true religion are more precious than gold and silver.'

Sepúlveda did not overlook the distinction established by the Scholastic philosophers between strict servitude in the legal sense and natural servitude; and it was easy for him, in the dialogue, to throw these differences into relief.

The tireless Leopoldo asks Democrates, 'Do you think that the jurists (who also give importance to natural law in many things) are being ironical when they say that all men were born free from the beginning and that servitude was introduced against nature and merely under the law of nations?'

In this way the writer skilfully introduces into the dialogue the idea of natural freedom.

But Democrates answers: 'I think the jurists are speaking seriously and with much wisdom; but this word "servitude" means a very different thing for legal experts and for philosophers; for the former, servitude is accidental, resulting from *force majeure* and the law of nations, sometimes also from civil law, whereas for the philosophers servitude means dullness of wit and inhuman or barbarous customs.'

Hence, the difference observed by the Scholastic writers between legal and natural servitude coincided with that observed by Sepúlveda between the respective systems of the jurists and the philosophers.

Following on from this point, and referring to the practice adopted in Indo-America, the author makes a distinction between the fate of those natives who resisted the Spaniards and those who, out of prudence or fear, obeyed them. Just as the victor was entitled to determine the fate of the former—to allow them their freedom or not—according to his will, so, in the case of the latter, it would be unjust (not to say wicked and base) to reduce them to servitude and deprive them of their possessions. The only permissible course would be to keep them as subject liable to taxation, according to their nature and condition.

This again led to an intermediate or mixed system of government compromising between freedom and slavery, such as had been mentioned by earlier writers in an attempt to justify the *encomiendas*, the services rendered and the tributes paid by the Indians for the benefit of the Spaniards.

It is not surprising that Sepúlveda's reasoning was strongly approved by the *conquistadores* of Mexico, to the point that the *Ayuntamiento*, or municipal council, agreed to offer him 'something from this land in the form of jewels and raiment to the value of two hundred gold pesos'.

To sum up: Sepúlveda's doctrine upheld the notion of a tutelage exercised by the civilized over the barbarian, but not necessarily the notion of legal servitude.

The *Democrates alter* touches upon another aspect of the relationship between nations which is of undoubted interest to readers of our own day.

Leopoldo the German asks the following tricky question: 'What would happen if a prince, impelled not by greed or thirst for dominion, but by the smallness or the poverty of his own domain, were to make war upon his neighbours in order to seize their territory, as being an almost necessary prey?'

To which Democrates replies: 'That would not be war, but plain robbery'. This opinion was shared by Vitoria, who considered it idle to discuss the matter, since either side could advocate the same cause and the result would be not justice but chaos.

The doctrine of natural servitude, invoked in the controversy over the New World, gave rise to critical reactions from the Spanish Scholastics, who, basing their arguments on the idea of Christian freedom, **CHRISTIAN FREEDOM** pleaded for a more generous and pacific treatment of the Indians.

The first Dominicans landed on Hispaniola in 1510. On the Sunday before Christmas, Friar Antonio de Montesinos preached his famous sermon in defence of the Indians: 'I rise to speak to you here, as the voice of Christ in the desert of this island. . . . That voice proclaims that you are in mortal sin, that you are living and dying in such sin by reason of your cruelty and tyrannical behaviour towards these innocent people. . . . Are they not men? Have they not reasoning minds? . . .'

Words of this sort were displeasing to the authorities and to the settlers in the island. King Ferdinand the Catholic expressed his disapproval as soon as he was informed of them. So did the Superior of the Dominican Order in Spain, but with this reservation: if Friar Antonio's conscience forbids him to give way on the matter which has earned disapproval, he must return to Spain. This was done, and so began a campaign on behalf of the indigenous peoples of America which was destined to have repercussions both in the sphere of ideas and in the more practical sphere of government institutions.

Such was the state of affairs in the Antilles when Las Casas also came to the fore—a tireless 'Indians' advocate in the royal court' as one of his opponents called him.

Both in public councils and in private discussions, some Christian voice was always raised in defence of the indigenous peoples.

Outstanding minds in Spanish religious and university life became interested in the controversy, as can be seen from the spirited interventions of Vitoria, Soto, Vázquez de Menchaca, Acosta, Báñez, Suárez, etc.

Without going into details which lie outside the scope of the present study, we may trace in general outline the development of the liberal doctrine which was to form the basis of the statute adopted by Spain for the government of the indigenous peoples in the New World.

About the year 1512, when the Council of Burgos, to which reference has already been made, was meeting, one of its members, Friar Bernardo de Mesa, of the Order of Preachers, who supported the concept of natural servitude, had to deal with an important objection put forward by the champions of freedom for the Indians. Their argument was that the incapacity attributed to the Indians of America was in contradiction to the goodness and might of their Creator; for, when a cause produces an effect which is unfitted to achieve its objective, there must be some defect in the cause, and 'that would mean that it was a fault on the part of God to have created men not possessed of sufficient capacity to accept the Faith and be saved'.

Friar Bernardo recoiled in horror from this suggestion, and pointed out that no one in his senses could maintain that the Indians did not possess the capacity to receive the Christian faith and virtue that would suffice to save them and lead them to ultimate bliss. But he did venture to say that they showed so little disposition by nature and habit that it needed much effort to bring them to accept the Faith and to adopt a good way of life, as they were very far from being ready for it; and, even supposing that they did accept the Faith, their nature did not permit them to persevere in virtue. According to Mesa, it followed that, although the Indians were capable of receiving the Faith, it was nevertheless necessary to keep them in some form of servitude, so as to make them of better disposition and constrain them to perseverance; and this was consonant with God's goodness.

Here the hierarchy established by the classical writers, based on the theory of differing degrees of reason, came up against the teaching of the Bible concerning the creation of man by God: 'And God said, Let us make man in our image, after our likeness.... So God created man in his own image' (Genesis i, 26, 27). As an essential defect in the creature might imply a fault on the part of his Creator, Friar Bernardo found himself obliged to modify the idea of the supposed incapacity of the Indian: for in absolute terms such an idea was untenable, since it was possible for any man to accept the Faith and be saved. He had the belief that for geographical reasons and because of vicious habits the capacity of the Indian had been diminished; but the principle of rational human dignity to which he subscribed was more generous and optimistic than the degree of intellectual capability that Aristotle conceded the barbarians. By means of a typical Scholastic compromise, Mesa arrived at the opinion that this capacity to accept the Faith was compatible with some form of natural servitude based on defective powers of reasoning, here discreetly altered to mean unsuitable habits and little natural disposition for accepting and keeping to the Faith and for leading a good life.

Mesa tried to keep the balance between Aristotle and Genesis. Moreover, the appearance of the inhabitants of the New World upon the scene added to the gravity of these questions: was it possible that there should be so many new human beings who were irrational? To what extent could such irrationality be reconciled with the idea of a perfect Creation? How far down could one go in a scale of distinctions between human beings, without prejudice to the principles of Christian philosophy?

Explanations for the opposition between the Divine creation of man
and the defects of the earthly creature were usually found by Christian
thinkers either in the idea of nature—spoken of in the sixteenth century
as God's steward—liable to error, or in the distinction between the state
of innocence and that of the fallen world. However, the extent of the
problem raised by the alleged incapacity of the Indians explains the
appearance of the objections which Friar Bernardo de Mesa tried to
circumvent, without succeeding in putting an end to the controversy,
as we shall see later.

Like a barrister trying to impress the judge with an accumulation of
all the reasons in support of his case, Friar Bartolomé de Las Casas
(1474-1566) had recourse to various ideological arguments for the
purpose of protecting the Indians from the consequences of the doctrine
of natural servitude, and more particularly from war, slavery and the
encomienda system.

He began by analysing the situation as it was in fact: the Indians were
not irrational or barbarian, as was imagined by those who called
them serfs by nature. That was a calumny born of ignorance or of bad
faith and interested motives on the part of the informants. On the
contrary, they were possessed of reason, moral and political capability,
mechanical skill, good dispositions, and beauty of face and form. Many
of them could even be the superiors of the Spaniards in monastic,
economic and political life, and could teach them good habits; they could,
moreover, surpass them in natural reason, as the Philosopher had said
in speaking of the Greeks and barbarians.

Las Casas' opinions were not always at this level of exaltation, for he
came to recognize that the Indians had some defects which put them
outside the bounds of perfection and orderly living; but he compared
this state with the former state of all the nations of the world 'when men
first began to people the earth', and insisted that this did not mean that
the people of the New World were lacking in the reasoning powers
required to fit them for an orderly way of life, for intercourse and for
domestic and political activities.

The widespread practice of human sacrifice was an obstacle to
idealization of the culture of the Indians; nevertheless, our robust
Christian of the sixteenth century did not quail before the problem.
'Nations which offer human sacrifices to their gods', he stated, 'have
for that very reason a better idea and a loftier appreciation of the excellence, deity and merit (though they are deluded idolators) of those gods
for which they thus have a greater regard; they give proof of sounder
reasoning and judgement, and use the functions of understanding
better than all the others, and have an advantage over the others in that
they are more religious; they also surpass all other nations in the world
in that they offer their own sons as a sacrifice for the good of their people.'

This doctrine would not surprise modern anthropologists; but to Sepúlveda, in his dispute with Las Casas, it seemed 'wicked and heretical'.

Another essential aspect of Las Casas' theory was his way of explaining the 'intention' of Aristotle in upholding the doctrine of natural servitude.

On one occasion, Las Casas asserted that the just-mentioned doctrine related to civil government rather than to slavery; in other words, that the Philosopher merely wished to explain that nature provided the world with some specially capable men so that they might be able to govern the others.

But, as Friar Bartolomé was aware that the theory of servitude had been explained in that part of the *Politics* which concerned the administration of the family, he had to accept as 'another' teaching of Aristotle 'that, in order to meet the requirements of the two combinations or partnerships necessary to a house, namely husband and wife and master and serf, nature had provided some natural serfs—erring from perfection in such a way as to make them lacking in the necessary judgement to govern themselves by reason and giving them bodily strength to enable them to serve the master of the house—an arrangement by which advantage would accrue both to them, as serfs by nature, and to those who, being endowed with wisdom to rule over the house, were by nature their masters.'

This explanation was closer to the Aristotelian conception of natural servitude, although, as we have seen, Las Casas was careful to specify that the type of servitude in question occurred when, by 'an error of nature', men were born lacking the necessary judgement to govern themselves by reason. We shall refer again later to the origin and scope of this important addition to the theory. Then followed the usual assertion that the said servitude was not applicable to the Indians, because they were not lacking in reason and judgement to govern their own houses and those of others.

Another device to which Las Casas had recourse in his endeavours to protect the Indians from the effects of the Aristotelian doctrine of servitude, consisted in drawing a distinction between different categories of barbarians. In general, those peoples who had some singularity in their opinions or customs—though they might not be lacking in wisdom to govern themselves—were considered barbarians. Others were so considered because they were illiterate. But, concerning these two types, Las Casas observed that Aristotle never meant to convey that they were serfs by nature and that therefore it was permissible to make war upon them. The classical argument, Friar Bartolomé believed, was only applicable to a third category of barbarians who, owing to the depravity of their ways, their lack of skill and brutish inclinations, were like wild beasts, living without towns or houses, without a police system, without laws, without ceremonies or dealings compatible with the *jus gentium*; but wandering about *palantes*, as the Latin says—in fact, engaging in robbery and violence. Concerning such persons one could agree with Aristotle that, just as it was legitimate to hunt wild beasts, so it was fair to make war upon them, in self-defence and in an endeavour to bring them to an orderly way of life. But the Indians were a gregarious and civil people and sufficiently orderly for it not to be permissible, on the grounds of a barbarian condition, to make war upon them.

In this way, Las Casas reconciled the anthropological fact (more favourable than that accepted by his opponents) with a conception of barbarianism divided into convenient types, in order to reduce Aristotle's theory to what he thought it ought to mean.

Freedom of interpretation enabled the Scholastic thinker to surround the pagan doctrine with so many distinctions and conditions, that it came to mean what suited its interpreter, and not what Aristotle, the sage of classical culture, had believed.

With regard to the authority of Aristotle, another question arose which deserves attention: what validity had the doctrine of a pagan sage for Christians? Were the admirable men of the ancient world, who died before the coming of Christ, spiritually lost or saved? Was their doctrine compatible with the Christian faith?

It should be noted that the attitude of Christian thinkers in the sixteenth century to the classical argument of natural servitude depended upon the way in which this major question was answered.

Sepúlveda thought that, generally speaking, the Aristotelian doctrine differed little—if at all—from the Christian, and he was confident that Aristotle would be found among the blessed.

Las Casas, on the other hand, stressed the Philosopher's pagan state and believed that he was 'burning in hell'. He recommended that his doctrine should only be used where it conformed to the Holy Faith and custom of the Christian religion. Accordingly, in respect of the conflict between the classical hierarchy and Christian freedom, Friar Bartolomé disengaged himself from the authority of the Philosopher in order to propound the following high principle: 'Our Christian religion is equal and adaptable to all nations of the world; it receives all men equally and takes from no one his freedom or his possessions, or places him in servitude, on the pretext that men are either slaves by nature or free by nature.'

This independence *vis-à-vis* Aristotle's authority was not exceptional, as may be seen from other pronouncements by Spanish writers of the sixteenth and seventeenth centuries.

For instance, Bartolomé de Albornoz, in a controversy concerning the enslavement of Negroes, stated that the war that was being waged against the Negroes was not just, either according to Aristotle, 'or—much

39

less so, indeed—according to Jesus Christ, whose philosophy is different from that of others'.

Returning to Las Casas' theory, it is necessary to revert to the objection which preoccupied Friar Bernardo de Mesa, that is to say, the incompatibility that existed between the irrationality of the Indians and the idea of the Divine creation of man.

We have already seen that Las Casas only admitted that it was by 'an error of nature' that some men existed who lacked the reasoning powers necessary to govern themselves. The exceptional nature of this state of 'amentia' was explained on the grounds that, in Las Casas' opinion, mankind as a product of the Creation was normally endowed with reason. Consequently, he said that serfs were by nature feeble-minded, incapable and lacking in reasoning power: 'they are thus like monsters among mankind, and such must be very few in number and seldom found'. Exceptionally, a man or an animal may be born with only one leg, or one arm, or one eye, or with more than two, or with six fingers. The same happens with trees, and 'among other created things, which are always born and continue perfect according to their species, and there is very seldom found a monstrosity among them, which is said to be an error on the part of nature; to a yet lesser extent do abnormalities occur among human kind, even in the physical sphere, and necessarily to a very much lesser extent in the realm of the understanding; for, then, abnormality means madness, feeble-mindedness or idiocy, and that is the greatest monstrosity that can occur, since the main characteristic of mankind is to be endowed with reason—a fact which places him above all other created things, with the exception of the angels.'

Las Casas thought that those men who, exceptionally, were lacking in the powers of reasoning required to enable them to govern themselves were the ones who could be considered serfs by nature; and, as the Indians were found to be so numerous, 'it is thus impossible, even if we had not seen the contrary with our own eyes, that they could be serfs by nature and, therefore, monsters among mankind, since nature always works perfectly and does not err except in the very smallest degree.'

In other words, according to this sixteenth-century religious thinker, who accepts the Biblical teaching concerning the creation of the world by God, reason, the distinctive characteristic of the human race, cannot be lacking in man to any numerical extent or in any degree.

In the passage quoted above, Las Casas sets aside all considerations of fact. The anthropology of the American native is discreetly relegated to the background; on the other hand, prominence is give to the *a priori* idea of the rationality of mankind, and to the tendency of any species to conserve the attributes with which it was invested by the Divine act of creation. The fact that the Indians were so numerous suffices to make the argument of irrationality inapplicable to them. We may recall in this connexion the phrase: 'it is thus impossible, even if we had not seen the contrary with our own eyes, that they could be serfs by nature. . . .'

However, so as to dispel any doubt, Las Casas adds, in the *Apologética Historia*, that to call all or most of the peoples of the New World barbarian and irrational is to accuse the Divine work of a major error, which nature and its order could not tolerate: 'As if the Divine Providence, in creating a countless number of rational minds, had become neglectful of its task and allowed errors to occur in the human species, on behalf of which it had resolved to do so much, and, in regard to a vast section of mankind, had acted in such a way, that all these people turned out to be non-social beings and therefore monsters, contrary to the natural inclination of all the peoples of the world.'

From this basic idea of creation Las Casas draws the conclusion that there is an essential unity of mankind: 'all the nations of the world are men, and for each and all of them there is only one definition: all have understanding and will; all have five external senses and four internal, by which they are motivated; all rejoice in the good and have pleasure in what is delightful and joyful, and all reject and abhor evil and are hostile towards what is disagreeable and harmful.'

Applying this principle to religious questions, he affirms: 'There never was any generation, or race, or people, or language among all created men—and even more so since the Redemption—that could not be counted among the predestined, that is to say, members of the mystical Body of Christ, the Church, as St. Paul said.'

In accordance with this idea of man, Las Casas had faith in the capacity of all uncivilized peoples to become civilized. He did not believe in a permanent and unchangeable barbarianism: 'Just as untilled land yields only thorns and thistles, but still has virtue in itself so that, when tilled, it produces good fruits in their season, so, all men throughout the world, however barbarian and brutal they may be, can, since they are men, attain to the use of reason and the understanding of matters pertaining to instruction and doctrine; it therefore follows inevitably that there can be no man in the world, however barbarian and inhuman, nor any nation which, if taught in the manner appropriate to the natural condition of men, more especially as regards the doctrine of the Faith, does not produce the reasonable fruits of excellence.'

This theological faith in human progress, as reflected in the course of history, led Las Casas to conclude: 'although in the beginning men were all uncivilized, like untilled land, and wild and bestial, yet, through the discretion and ability innate in their minds, God having created them rational beings, once they are brought under control and persuaded by reason and love and industriousness—which is the proper way to influence rational creatures and bring them to the exercise of virtue—there is not and cannot be any nation incapable of being converted and brought to full political virtue and the full measure of civilized political and rational men.'

Accordingly, the idea of the Divine creation of mankind safeguarded its rationality and counteracted the idea of 'amentia' on which natural servitude was based. There might be aggressive men, violent in their ways (the *palantes*); exceptionally there might be men lacking in reason; and 'in the beginning' uncivilized ways, ferocity and bestiality might prevail; but amentia could not extend to whole peoples, in any degree, nor could the uncivilized be devoid of the capacity for improvement. To be convinced, it was not necessary to wait to see this with one's own eyes, but only to believe it with Christian understanding, which implied belief in the powerful and just work of the Creator. 'All the peoples of the world are men'—not some of them men and others inferior beings, as Sepúlveda would have it.

In spite of his habitual exaggerations, Las Casas succeeded in giving expression to the doctrine of Christian freedom which served to protect the rights of the Indian.

A striking reflexion of this thought is to be found in the famous Bull of Pope Paul III, of 9 June 1537. With an authority in the Christian world that the opinions of the authors of treatises lacked, it stated: 'We know that this same Truth, which can neither deceive nor be deceived, when it sent the Preachers of the faith to perform this mission, said: "go forth and teach all men"; go to all men, indiscriminately, for all are capable of receiving the teaching of our faith . . . these same Indians, as true men . . . are capable of receiving the Christian faith . . . we declare that these Indians and all other peoples who from now onward may come to the notice of Christians, even though they may be outside the Christian faith, are not, and should not be, deprived of their freedom or of control over their possessions . . . they should be attracted to, and persuaded to embrace, the Christian faith. . . .'

The serene confidence with which it is stated that all men are capable of receiving the teaching of the faith and that they should not lose their freedom or their possessions, surpasses any notion founded on experience, for it applies both to the Indians already discovered and to 'all other peoples who from now onward may come to the notice of Christians'.

We shall not follow these ideas through the writings of each of the great Scholastic thinkers of the sixteenth and seventeenth centuries who concerned themselves with the problems of the American continent; nor shall we refer to the frequent official assemblies at which they were discussed. But it does seem necessary to draw attention to the principles which, issuing from various sources, went to make up the body of doctrine that finally served as the basis for the laws governing Indo-America.

Does their natural environment condemn certain peoples to irrationality and subjection?

We have already seen that the first Scholastics who were consulted on the case of the Indians, such as well as Juan Ginés de Sepúlveda, endeavoured to explain the incapacity of the people of the New World on geographical grounds, such as the latitude, the fact that they were island-dwellers, and the influence of the stars.

Others writers, including Las Casas and Gregorio López, the latter in 1555, maintained that experience did not justify this supposed causality. López stated that near the equator many peoples were living in pleasant, fertile and temperate lands. And we have seen that Las Casas opposed the geographical theory that was unfavourable to the peoples of the Antilles by making pertinent comparisons with island-dwellers near to Europe.

The controversy was dominated by political and moral, rather than scientific, interests. The modern mind finds little of anthropological value in these disputes concerning the barbarian condition of the Indians. It is, however, important to note that account was taken of the influence of environment on human civilization, and that from that approach ensued political consequences which affected the peoples of those remote regions.

This was not to be the last time that a problem of colonial expansion was related to theories concerning climate and other natural phenomena. Like the advocates of servitude in the sixteenth century, later writers invoked the science of nature, held in such esteem for its strict truth, in order to spare themselves many of the ethical and juridical preoccupations arising from contacts with different civilizations.

As we have seen, the Spanish Scholastic writers finally chose the ethical explanation and abandoned the attractions and expediency of the arguments based on the determining influence of natural factors.

Is barbarianism a uniform state justifying the use of violence to bring the barbarians into subjection or should a distinction be drawn between different categories of barbarians deserving different treatment?

It was the Jesuit José de Acosta (d. 1600) who perfected the division of the barbarians into different categories, already begun by Las Casas. Instead of agreeing with Sepúlveda's view that the Indians all belonged to one and the same barbarian group, he tried to demonstrate by his theory the diversity of the cultures obtaining in the New World. Including within his classification the peoples of both America and Asia, he divided the barbarians into three types: (a) those who did not diverge to any great extent from the true reason and customs of human kind; this category consisted mainly of those who had a body politic, laws, fortified towns, magistrates, wealthy and regular trade, and—above all—

who used the art of writing: such, for instance, as the Chinese, Japanese and other peoples of the East Indies; these should be persuaded, without the use of force, to embrace the Christian faith; (b) barbarians who, though illiterate and not possessing written laws or philosophical and political writings nevertheless had a real magistrature and a body politic, settled dwellings, a police system, leaders and military and religious orders—who in fact, to a certain extent, governed themselves by means of human reason. These included the Mexicans and Peruvians, who had admirable institutions. However, they did diverge to a considerable extent from the true reason and customs of human kind. Acosta was not opposed to placing those of them who entered the Christian fold under the rule of Christian princes and magistrates, but he considered that they should be allowed to retain such of their rights, possessions and laws as were not contrary to nature or to the teaching of the Scriptures; (c) the last category of barbarians did not include all the inhabitants of the New World: it consisted of the savages who lived like wild beasts, scarcely possessing human feelings, without laws, kingdoms or alliances, without a real magistrature or a body politic, without settled dwellings (or, if they had dwellings, these were more like wild beasts' caves or stables). He mentioned the Caribbean peoples as examples of this category of barbarians, and held that Aristotle's view that such could be subdued by force, like wild animals, applied in their case. However, if serious error were to be avoided and if the Gospel were not to be presented as an invitation to greed and tyranny, this method was not acceptable in respect of all the Indians.

The main outcome of these distinctions was to limit the range of subjugation by force to a certain type of barbarians and to strengthen the rights of those placed under Christian rule.

Does barbarianism result from natural incapacity or from a wrong upbringing? In other words, is it an intrinsic attribute of human nature or a state capable of being changed by religious and cultural methods?

The usual answer of the Spanish thinkers was that the barbarian could be educated. In 1539, Vitoria said of the Indians: 'The fact that they seem so imbecile is largely due to a wrong upbringing, just as, among our own people, there are many rustics that differ little from the animals.' Towards the middle of the same century, Gregorio López asserted that the incapacity of the Indians was due more to the fact that they were infidels than to a lack of human reason. The jurist Solórzano Pereira, writing in 1629, took up this idea, in referring to those who were endeavouring to prove that any man, however savage, provided he had some spark of reason, could, with patience, be educated and instructed.

This assertion, deeply rooted in Christian thought, was linked up with the idea of the Divine creation of man, as we have noted in considering Las Casas' thought. Vitoria, too, maintained that 'God and nature do not fall short in what is necessary for the majority of the species, and the principal attribute of man is reason, and power that does not culminate in action is vain.' That is to say, the irrationality which serves as a basis for the notion of natural servitude, if it goes beyond the margin of 'exception', calls in question the Divine and natural order which presupposes capability in the majority of mankind. In a work dedicated to Charles V, written in 1552, López de Gómara stated that in the New World, 'the people are like us, except for their colour, for otherwise they would be beasts and monsters, and not, as they are, descendants of Adam.' This pronouncement is accompanied by another, of undoubted practical significance: 'It is right that men who are born free should not be the slaves of other men, especially when as the result of Holy Baptism they are freed from the servitude of the Devil, even though, according to the learned saints Augustine and Chrysostom, servitude and captivity are punishment and penalty for sin.'

Can legal and natural servitude be regarded as identical, or are there such differences between them that a distinction can be made between the fate of people in one or the other situation?

Aristotle made a distinction between servitude imposed by law—for instance, as a result of war—and what he termed natural servitude in that it arose from the inequalities between men as regards the use of reason. It will be remembered that Sepúlveda similarly maintained that servitude had a very different meaning for the jurist and for the philosopher. However, it was left to the Spanish Scholastic writers, who had not forgotten the tradition of the jurists of the Middle Ages, to draw the final conclusions from the distinction between the two kinds of servitude, with the frank intention of liberalizing the concept of natural servitude.

Among others, Fernando Vázquez de Menchaca (d. 1569), Domingo Báñez (d. 1604) and Diego de Saavedra Fajardo (in a work written in 1631) affirmed that natural servitude did not correspond to what the name suggested; that it was beneficial to the serf and therefore was not in fact a servitude; nor, to be precise, should it so be called, 'except in a wide and general sense of the term'. Natural serfs were free in everything, and they served wise men in order to receive guidance from them and not for their masters' advantage.

Vitoria's view was that the nature of the tutelage of the wise man over the barbarian was similar to the tutelage exercised over minors and the feebleminded; it might be based on charity, since it was for the good of the ward and not only for the profit of the guardian. Domingo de Soto (d. 1560) agreed with him in this, and said: 'the man who is a master by nature does not make use of natural serfs as things he possesses for his own advantage, but as free men with their own rights, for their good —that is to say, by teaching them and inculcating good habits in them.'

45

Solórzano Pereira, in the century following the Conquest, even repeated that such tutelage was intended to be more to the advantage of the barbarian than to that of the wise man, and that the governance o Indians who had some degree of culture should be political and no despotic, for they were free men by nature.

This trend in Scholastic ideas marked the close of the period o Christian revision of classical imperialism; for, although Aristotle had admitted that natural servitude brought with it some benefits for the man who was incapable of governing himself, he did not conceal the fac that it operated mainly to the advantage of the master. Nor should we forget that at the beginning of the colonial era the Spaniards accepted the idea of a type of government for Indians which was a compromise between servitude and freedom. Next came a more generous interpre tation of the status and destiny of the peoples of America; for, according to the doctrine of the revisionist Scholastics, the men of the Old World should go to the New with the intention of teaching the Indians a religiou and civilized way of life, endeavouring in charity to act for their good and enjoying the material benefits only incidentally to the purpose of their paternal and Christian mission.

This was a theory—no more, but also no less. For we must not overlook the fact that there was an attempt at justice and generosity in the intention; nor must we close our eyes to the extreme oppression that migh have obtained in the absence of this liberal Christianity, which—allowing for the circumstances of the times—did represent that generosity and urge for freedom which, fortunately, have characterized men at al periods of history.

But what, if any, were the practical results of this doctrine?

After some fluctuations, the laws applying to Indo-America prohibited the enslavement of the indigenous peoples; accordingly, about th middle of the sixteenth century, the captives of the conquests and war were freed. In the courts of Mexico City alone, freedom was granted to over three thousand Indians, not counting those emancipated in the provinces. Thereafter, servitude was only allowed in the case o unruly aborigines who maintained centres of hostility within th Empire.

The *encomiendas* were not abolished until the eighteenth century At first sight, this seemed to represent a triumph for the supporters o the theory of natural servitude; but it was openly declared that th Indian working on the *encomienda* was free and the institution itsel was reformed so as to bring it into conformity with the principle of civilizing Christian tutelage.

Many of the general provisions concerning the Indians, after th Conquest, were based on protective and humanitarian principles, whic are usually regarded as an honour to the Spanish rule in America. Fo instance, the *Recopilación de las Leyes de Indias* contains one complete section on 'good treatment of the Indians'.

As regards religion, Christianity was propagated among the native peoples on the implicit basis of human brotherhood in Christ. The duty of teaching them and receiving them into the faith was constantly stressed in official and ecclesiastical documents.

Civil education was provided by various means, such as the grouping together of Indians in townships, the changing of customs incompatible with those of Europe, the granting of legal rights and administrative guardianship aimed at affording protection.

Scholastic thought and its institutional manifestations naturally came up against the social reality of a colonization dominated by economic interests, in which context the harmonious co-existence of different races and cultures was hard to achieve. Such contacts are liable to give rise to clashes and excesses which neither theory nor law are always able to restrain. Nor could one expect to find in every ecclesiastic, official or colonist an apostle prepared to sacrifice himself for the conversion and welfare of the Indians. Exploitation and excesses were common occurrences in the lands under Spanish control.

But perhaps for this very reason the influence of liberal ideas in this colonization was more striking, for, far from offering mere academic or legal trappings, they provided the spiritual basis for an administrative system in the operation of which (given the prevailing circumstances) there was ample opportunity of appreciating their virtues as well as the factors limiting their application.

The loftiness and liberality of the aims thus pursued gave rise to a spirit of reform in the colonial institutions of Spanish America which, hitherto dominated by the desire for gain, then came under the influence of the higher principles of human dignity.

It was this which accounted for the development of the conflict between the utilitarianism of the *conquistadores* and the colonists, on the one hand, and the idea of guardianship over the Indians, on the other.

The ideological trend which favoured protection for the indigenous population of America also influenced the attitude towards the treatment of the Negro.

Some years ago, Professor Altamira drew attention to the early liberal theories propounded by certain Spanish thinkers of the sixteenth century on behalf of the Africans. However, this subject has not been sufficiently stressed in the historiography of the Americas, and it is appropriate to devote some attention to it here and even to look in detail at its origins.

In his *Historia de las Indias*, Bartolomé de Las Casas tells that, at the beginning and with the object of securing freedom for the Indians, he had advocated that the Spaniards should be permitted to bring Negroes to Indo-America; but later he regretted this, seeing the injustice of the way in which the Portuguese took them and made them slaves, and from that time onwards he spoke of their enslavement as unjust and tyrannical 'because they possess the same powers of reasoning as the Indians'.

Francisco de Vitoria, answering a question put to him by Friar Bernardino de Vique, made a distinction between the following cases: Negroes captured by trickery; those who were slaves as the result of wars between themselves; and those bought in commutation of the death sentence. He did not consider the first case justifiable and doubted whether it was a widespread practice, because, if so, it would compromise the conscience of the King of Portugal. As regards the second case, he admitted the idea that the Portuguese should buy these Negroes, for they were under no obligation to inquire into the justice of wars between barbarians: 'it is enough that the man is a slave, either in fact or in law, and I buy him outright'. He also admitted the third case.

He asked that slaves be treated humanely, because they were our neighbours, and both master and slave had another lord (God); provided they were well treated, they were better off as slaves than if they had been left in their own countries.

Concerning the question whether the belief that the King of Portugal and his Council would not allow unjust transactions provided a sufficient safeguard for the conscience, he did not think so, although he thought it improbable that the use of trickery as a means of capturing Negroes (attracting them with toys and then capturing them) was tolerated and commonly used.

With greater abolitionist zeal and admittedly influenced by the American Indian problem, Friar Alonso de Montúfar, Archbishop of Mexico City, a member of the Order of Preachers, wrote to the King of Spain on 30 June 1560: 'We do not know what reason there may be for Negroes to be captives any more than Indians for, according to what we hear, they willingly receive the Holy Gospel and do not make war upon Christians.' The fact that Negroes were sought as slaves served to encourage the wars that took place among the Negro peoples themselves, for thus they would have captives to sell. As to the material and spiritual benefits they derived from being the slaves of Christians, these were counteracted by the serious harm resulting from the separation of wives from husbands, children from parents. The Archbishop therefore asked for an explanation of the reasons for the enslavement of Negroes, so that his scruples might be removed. 'May it please Our Lord that this enslavement cease; and that, just as men have hitherto gone out to trade in the bodies of these people, so henceforward they may be more concerned to preach to them the Holy Gospel, that in their

)wn lands, they may thus live free, not only in their bodies but even
nore in their souls, through a true knowledge of Jesus Christ.'

In 1569, Friar Tomás de Mercado published his work entitled *Tratos
) Contratos de Mercaderes*, intended especially for the merchants of
Seville. Chapter XV deals with the Cape Verde trade in Negro slaves and
here, as in the other parts of the work, the author analyses the moral
consequences which may ensue for the consciences of the Spanish
merchants.

In his opinion, it is lawful and in conformity with the *jus gentium* to
capture or sell Negroes or any other people, this being on a par with
he division and distribution of goods, and he considers that there are
sufficient grounds to justify the capture and sale of men. Concerning
he Negroes, he mentions: (a) the wars that they often wage among
hemselves because, like the Italians, they are not under the rule of one
universal master; (b) the punishment of crimes by loss of liberty, a
practice also current among the Indians; (c) in cases of extreme necessity,
he sale of children by their parents, as happens in Guinea.

After establishing the lawfulness of the situation, Mercado goes on to
examine the facts. He finds that innumerable abuses are committed in
he following connexions: some Negroes hunt others in order to sell
hem; some overlords punish their subjects out of anger, and not for
reasons of justice; parents sell their children without being forced
o do so by necessity. There is also trickery on the part of the Europeans
vho go to buy Negroes, and the Negroes purchased are ill-treated while
peing transported from one place to another.

For the above reasons, Mercado, showing a remarkably advanced
humanitarian outlook, contrasts the facts of the situation with the
doctrine, and advises Spanish merchants not to take part in the slave
trade, however lawful this may be in itself. He points out that the Negroes
ose their freedom for ever, and that this is a serious and irreparable
injury. He likens the behaviour of a Spanish merchant who does business
vith the Portuguese or Negro slave traders to that of an old-clothes
dealer who buys goods which he has reason to suppose are stolen,
vhich is a punishable offence. If a purchase is to be lawful, the buyer
must be sure that the object bought belongs to the seller or, at least,
hat there is no indication to the contrary. The idea of having persons
of confidence, to examine cases, stationed in the Cape Verde Islands,
does not seem to him likely to lead to satisfactory results; it is preferable
o desist from the slave trade. Some people are of opinion that, as the
King of Portugal has a Council, it is for this body to define the question
of conscience; but Mercado states that the theologians of Seville and
Castile asked the theologians of Lisbon whether they approved of the
lave trade, and the latter replied by asking whether the Sevillians
and Castilians thought that theology was different in Lisbon and saying

that they, in Lisbon, condemned the trade just as the Spanish theologian did. Does the fault lie with the King of Portugal? Mercado presume that his ordinances are good; but—as in the case of the Spaniards—i may happen that ordinances are not always carried out.

Bartolomé de Albornoz, after a long stay in New Spain, expresses himself in similar terms in his *Arte de Contratos*, published in Valenci in 1573.

He approved of the traffic as far as the Moors of Barbary, Tripol and Cyrenaica were concerned because they in turn captured Christians but he opposed the trade in Negroes from Ethiopia.

He condemned those who commissioned ships on their own authorit and stole slaves, or who bought stolen slaves; it was contrary to ever law, divine and human, to molest anyone who was causing no harm, an even worse to enslave him. When the trade was carried on through th intermediary of the Portuguese, who trafficked in Negro slaves with th authorization of their King, selling them publicly and paying charge therefor, some people held that this involved no transgression agains the law since the sovereign allowed it, and no transgression agains conscience since it was done publicly and the priests did not forbi it as they had done in the case of the Indians—indeed, they even bough Negro slaves themselves. But Albornoz did not admit this opinion 'for these wretched Ethiopians have committed no offence to warran loss of liberty, and there are no public or private grounds (howeve evident they may seem) which suffice to exculpate those who hold then in servitude, usurping their freedom.'

Negroes could become Christians without being slaves; freedom o the soul did not have to be paid for by enslavement of the body; it wa better to go to them as apostles for the purpose of bringing then redemption and not to deprive them of the freedom which God ha given them by nature.

Opinions similar to the foregoing were expressed by Domingo de Soto Alonso de Sandoval, Luis de Molina y Diego de Avendaño.

And so we find that there were some who examined the situatio fairly on the basis of Christian premises and who dared to arrive a liberal conclusions favourable to Negroes, as others had done earlie in respect of the Indians. Several of the writers quoted had in min the experience of Indo-America and realized the absurdity of grantin freedom to the inhabitants of one continent to enslave those of anothe However, as Altamira pointed out: 'Their voices were lost in the voi and Negroes were brought freely into all parts of Indo-America.'

It is not easy to explain just how this came about. Perhaps th Portuguese example, to which reference is made on various occasion by Spanish writers, had some influence in the matter. It is also possibl that the Court considered the problem to be outside its jurisdictio since the lands of Africa were not the object of Spanish colonization as were those of Indo-America. In addition, mercantile interests were involved, and such interests were strong enough to outweigh the views of those theologians and jurists who had come to see the problem clearly.

The facts of the case were that the Spanish possessions in America received a considerable number of African slaves and that the principal nations of Europe took part in the slave trade.

What can be said with certainty is that the sixteenth-century tradition of Christian natural law, favourable to the Negro, was not entirely overlooked by writers in the Spanish language and in fact came to be incorporated in the philosophy of the eighteenth century.

The Mexican Jesuit Francisco Xavier Alegre (1729-88) speaks of the slave trade which had been carried on by the Portuguese in Africa since they occupied the Cape Verde Islands in about 1448; he says that after the discovery of America and the prohibition, by the most humane and saintly laws of Charles V and Philip II, of personal serfdom for the indigenous inhabitants, 'some persons recommended to the King that Ethiopian slaves should be sent to those new lands. And so those good men, imbued with zeal for the things of God, but not with a zeal inspired and enlightened by reason, whilst protecting the freedom of the American Indians, imposed upon the nations of Africa perpetual deportation and the cruel yoke of slavery.' This prior explanation enabled the writer to conclude: 'Therefore, since these Ethiopians were not slaves by birth, did not sell themselves and were not sold by their parents for reasons of pressing need, were not sentenced to slavery by a lawful judge, and cannot be regarded as captives in a just war (as their barbarous little kings fight among themselves out of mere caprice or for trifling reasons); since, moreover, from the time the Europeans embarked on the slave trade, they make war more often than before solely for the purpose of capturing men to sell, as is evident from the stories told by the Portuguese, English and Dutch themselves (the latter, in particular, engaging enthusiastically in the trade); it follows that such slavery, as Molina expressly stated, is entirely unjust and iniquitous, unless the Royal Ministers charged with this matter are informed of just rights which make it lawful in particular cases and testify thereto; especially if we reflect that in the kingdoms of Angola and the Congo, in St. Thomas' Island and other places, there are many Christians who have been captured by the infidels and it is not lawful for Christians to buy them. . . .'

Did the theory put foward by Alegre owe more to the 'zeal inspired and enlightened by reason' which he mentions in his discourse or to the quotation from Molina? It seems to show that the Scholastic trend of thought was already blending with the rationalist; but what is significant is that a Spanish American liberal of the eighteenth century should find a *point d'appui* in his own tradition.

As we have seen, there is no doubt that the Christian impulse was unable to check the enslavement of Negroes; it fell to the philosophy of Enlightenment to wage the decisive battle. But when the time came to associate Scholastic liberalism with eighteenth-century philosophy as Alegre did, the Christian tradition was able to help in diminishing the severity, generally speaking, of the treatment accorded to Negroes in Spanish colonial society, as was observed by travellers who had occasion to compare this régime with that obtaining in other European dependencies.

In the eighteenth century, the Encyclopaedist movement made its mark upon the counsels of the Spanish Government and the laws concerning Negroes, as is shown in the circular Order of 15 August 1789 on the education, treatment and use of slaves in Spanish America.

In later years, when the enslavement of African Negroes was abolished the humanitarian tradition had another beneficent task to perform to diminish the social prejudice which the enduring institution of slavery had left in its wake.

To sum up: the intellectual attitude of the Spaniards towards the treatment of the Indians and Negroes presents, on the one hand, limitations due to the times and the circumstances, and on the other, generous and universal ideas of human freedom which played their part in improving the condition of people belonging to cultures different from those of Europe.

It may therefore be said, without fear of falling into any false apologia that, from the beginning, slavery and freedom have waged in our midst their endless conflict, the outcome of which in each succeeding period of history has determined the degree of progress in ideas and practice which that period has handed down as a legacy to the living generation

From the eighteenth century onwards, new ideas arose concerning the equality and freedom of mankind.

EQUALITY IN THE EIGHTEENTH CENTURY

They were not a mere prolongation of sixteenth-century thought. The historical climate and even the subject-matter were different; but the new conclusions sometimes offered surprising resemblances to those of the Spanish polemists.

Theories concerning the New World were presented in various ways in eighteenth-century works: the Conquest and the enslavement of Indians and Negroes were censured; the enlightenment of the century was contrasted with the obscurantism of Spanish action (the terrifying example refered to by Raynal); there were discussions upon the degeneration of the species in the New World as compared with the Old; people talked of the youthfulness of the New World, in the dual sense of immaturity on the one hand and promise on the other; the type of man born in that corner of the earth, whether Indian, mestizo or creole, was either criticized or praised; America was cited in support of the theory of the 'noble savage', although the actual sight of the natives of South America led the French scientist La Condamine to conclude that 'left solely to nature, deprived of education and society, man differs little from the beasts'. In short, during a century of universal disturbance and revolutionary applications of natural law, America was not relegated to the background.

Subjects of such wide range fall outside the scope of the present paper; they have, in any case, a literature of their own.

We shall therefore confine ourselves to considering eighteenth-century attitudes with regard to the equality and freedom of the peoples of America.

In the first place, we still find echoes of the dispute concerning the reasoning powers of the Indian, which had aroused such passionate interest in the earlier polemists.

In his *Recherches Philosophiques sur les Américains*, published in Berlin in 1768, the well-read writer Cornelius de Pauw ventured to interpret the famous Bull of Pope Paul III on the capacity of the Indians in the following way: 'The inhabitants of America were thought at first to be not men but satyrs or large monkeys, that could be killed without remorse or blame. Finally, adding a touch of the ridiculous to the disasters of those times, a Pope issued an original Bull, in which he stated that, desiring to found bishoprics in the richest provinces of America, it pleased him and the Holy Spirit to acknowledge the Americans as real men. Without this decision by an Italian, there would thus, to this day, still be doubt in the minds of the faithful whether the inhabitants of the New World were in fact men. There is no other example of

53

such a decision since this globe has been inhabited by men and monkeys.'

Similarly, in his *History of America* (1777), the historian Robertson recounted that some missionaries, astonished at the dull-wittedness and insensibility of the Indians, described them as so degenerate as to be incapable of understanding the first rudiments of religion; and that a council held in Lima decreed that owing to their lack of mental powers they should be excluded from the sacrament of the Eucharist. Robertson acknowledged that Paul III, in his Bull of 1537, had declared them to be rational creatures capable of all the privileges of Christians. But, after two centuries, their progress in knowledge had been so slight that very few of them possessed the required intellectual discernment to be judged worthy of approaching the Holy Table. Even after the most continuous instruction, their belief was considered weak and questionable; and although some of them had succeeded to an extraordinary extent in studying learned languages and had completed academic courses with distinction, the weakness of their faith appeared still so suspect that no one of them had ever been ordained priest and very rarely had any been received into a religious order.

When writings of this kind by learned men in Europe came to the knowledge of people in America, they gave rise to strong hostile reactions.

Francisco Xavier Clavijero (1731-87) felt obliged to call de Pauw 'an author who is as malicious as he is an enemy of the truth'; for according to this Mexican Jesuit, the purpose of Paul III's Bull had not been 'to declare that the Americans were real men, but simply to defend their natural rights against the attacks of their persecutors, and to condemn the injustice and inhumanity of those who, on the pretext that these men were idolatrous or incapable of learning, deprived them of their possessions and their freedom and used them as beasts.' He stressed the fact that, before the Bull was issued, Ferdinand and Isabella had earnestly recommended that education should be provided for the Indians; had given very strict orders that they should be well treated and that no harm should be done to them as regards either their possessions or their freedom; and had sent many missionaries to them. The assertion that Paul III wished to recognize the Indians as real men in order to found bishoprics in the richest provinces of the New World, seemed to Clavijero 'a baseless calumny perpetrated by an enemy of the Roman Church'; 'such persons would do better to praise the zeal and humanity manifested by the Pope in the Bull in question'.

The attack against Robertson was no less vehement, for, in Clavijero's view, he had largely adopted 'the extravagant opinions of de Pauw'.

Clavijero himself had confidence in the intellectual capacity of the

American Indians, as also in the power of education to overcome so-called 'natural' obstacles.

In a passage in the *Historia Antigua de México*, published in 1780-81, he asserted, with regard to the Mexican Indians: 'Their minds are similar in every respect to those of the other sons of Adam, and they are endowed with the same faculties; Europeans never did so little honour to their own reason as when they cast doubts upon the rationality of the American Indians.'

In his *Disertaciones*, he added: 'After great experience and extensive study, which I feel qualifies me to judge with less risk of error, I solemnly affirm to de Pauw and to the whole of Europe that the minds of Mexicans are in no way inferior to those of Europeans; that they are capable of imbibing all knowledge, even the most abstract; and that, if serious attention were given to their education, if from childhood they were brought up in seminaries under good teachers and were cared for and encouraged by prizes, we should find among these Americans, philosophers, mathematicians and theologians who could compete with the most famous in Europe. But it is very difficult, not to say impossible, to make progress in learning when one lives a life of poverty, servitude and endless troubles.'

An awareness of the possible affinity between eighteenth-century ideas and those of the sixteenth-century Christians who upheld the theory of the capacity of the Indians and strove to defend their freedom is to be found in Clavijero's own remarks. Referring to the writings of de Pauw against the Indians, he allows himself the following ingenious play on words: 'He describes the Indians in such terms and speaks so insultingly of their minds that, although he is sometimes irritated by those who question their rationality, I do not doubt that if, at the time, he had been asked, he would have declared himself to be opposed to the views of the *rationalists*.' The last word is underlined in his text, no doubt to stress the intention to apply it, according to the linguistic fashion of the eighteenth century, to those theologians and men of letters of the time of the Conquest who upheld the theory that the Indian was a rational being, and incidentally to show how far the Prussian philosopher had departed from the canons of the Enlightenment in describing the inhabitants of Indo-America.

This faith in the capacity of the Indian and in the virtue of education was widespread in the Spanish-speaking world, as can be seen from the works of other writers of the time.

Among those living in the Peninsula, mention should be made of Joseph Campillo de Cossio, whose treatise on the *Nuevo sistema de gobierno económico para la América*, published in Madrid in 1789, had already been completed in 1743, the year of the author's death.

Concerning the incapacity of the Indians, he stated that it could not

be so great as many people were inclined to pretend, some even denyin
that they were rational beings. This seemed to him contrary to th
truth and based either on ignorance or on malice. The life of th
Indians before they came into contact with the Europeans showe
that they had remarkable talent and wisdom: 'This is very evident fror
their large cities, their splendid buildings, their powerful empire
their ordered way of living, under wise civil and military laws, with thei
own form of worship; and even now we can see how they imitate th
ablest Europeans in all the arts and crafts, with great skill. . . .' Campill
not only mistrusted those who described the Indians as lacking in power
of thought and reason, but was even prepared to maintain that they ha
'well balanced reasoning powers, definite capabilities and an under
standing, ability and aptitude neither so barbarian nor so unrefine
as is asserted'. Had the Indians at the time been what they were repre
sented to be, he suggests that extensive oppression could have reduce
them to barbarianism, as had been the case with the Greeks in their time
the descendants of those great captains, philosophers and statesmen wh
had once been masters of the world. In any case, however, there was n
objection to making the Indians useful vassals, within the meanin
Campillo gave to the term, as in a monarchy it was not necessary fo
everyone to discourse or to be highly talented. It was enough for th
majority to know how to work; only a few needed to command, and
was these who required to be specially gifted; the masses did not nee
anything more than bodily strength and docility to let themselves b
governed.

This was not an altruistic acknowledgement of the reasoning power
of the Indian. What interested Campillo, as a politician in the age (
enlightened despotism, was that the Indians should become 'usefu
vassals' of the Spanish monarchy—they should be good peasant
shepherds, etc., such as existed in the more cultured nations of Europ
He therefore found it expedient to defend the capacity of the America
Indians to perform these economic functions, which were essenti
to the maintenance and progress of society.

Antonio de Ulloa, in his *Relación Histórica del Viage a la Améric
Meridional*, published in Madrid in 1748, was more disinterested whe
he wrote: 'Much of the crudeness observed in the minds of these Indiar
derives from their lack of culture; for in some parts where they enjo
the benefits of education, they are found to be as rational as other men

The Mexican creole Juan José de Eguiara y Eguren, in the prologu
to his *Bibliotheca Mexicana*, printed in 1755, refuted, at length, th
arguments of the Dean of Alicante, Don Manuel Martí, who had writte
disdainfully of the culture of the New World. Full of indignation, h
tried to prove that the Indians could not be called rough and unculturec
and as for the American descendants of Europeans, he maintained tha

they were of outstanding intelligence, because the physical environment was favourable, among other reasons, and that they had a particular bent and love for learning. Following after Feijóo, he, too, addressed himself to demolishing the mistaken theory that although the Americans were endowed with precocious talent, they lost the use of it prematurely.

The Peruvian creole José Eusebio de Llano Zapata, in his *Memorias Histórico-phísico-crítico-apologéticas de la América Meridional*, dated 1761, in his turn censured Las Casas for the calumnies that had occasioned the discredit unjustly thrown upon the Spanish nation by the pens of foreign writers; but he did not on that account support Sepúlveda, whose book on the Indians seemed to him 'unsound, un-Christian and in complete disaccord with the dogmas of the Church'. He believed that the Indians had the same aptitudes for the arts and sciences 'as all other peoples of the ancient world', and that their imperfections were due 'not to defects in their capacity but to lack of education'.

These appreciations seem to derive from the observation and rationalism of the times rather than from the theology or politics of the sixteenth century, but essentially they are in agreement with Scholastic principles.

As regards the controversy concerning servitude, de Pauw himself accused Las Casas of having written 'a large number of reports intended to prove that the conquest of America was a colossal injustice and at the same time aimed at destroying the Africans, by means of slavery. . . .' The Prussian writer was surprised that Sepúlveda had not reproached his opponent for producing this odious report, '. . . so confused were ideas at that time; fanaticism, cruelty, and vested interests had perverted the early notions of the *jus gentium*'.

This accusation against Las Casas greatly preoccupied the thinkers of the eighteenth century and gave rise to an abundant literature.

Writing at the end of the eighteenth century, Domingo Muriel, a Jesuit at the University of Córdoba de Tucumán, admitted the distinction between servitude in the strict sense and natural servitude. In his opinion the Jesuit Acosta had understood the idea of Aristotle and his interpreter Thomas Aquinas better than Pufendorf and before Heineccius, for he had recognized that it was not a question of ordinary servitude, but of political and perhaps also economic servitude, it being in the nature of things that the simple are controlled and corrected by the wise. This kind of servitude might be compared with the case of a child, needing a tutor or guardian although himself the owner of his fortune.

It is also interesting to note that Muriel drew a liberal conclusion favourable to the slave from the idea of natural equality, for he says: 'It is vain for the master to agree that the slave is by nature a man equal to himself if he has the right of life and death over his slave, or if even

57

though he kills the slave he commits no injustice with respect to him.'
He made use of this argument to reject the supposed right of the master
over the slave.

Muriel ventured to deny that Las Casas had had African slavery in
mind; in his opinion, Sepúlveda could not reproach him on that account.
He thought that Las Casas was not condemning the conquest of America
but merely the abuses committed individually by the victors, and that
these abuses had been vastly exaggerated. According to Muriel, what
Las Casas had proposed was that labourers should be sent out.

It is obvious that Muriel was not fully informed in the matter. In spite
of his habitual mistakes, de Pauw in this case was somewhat nearer to the
historical facts; moreover, in line with the opinion generally held by
the philosophers of the Enlightenment, he exalted the moral progress
of his own times by comparison with the sixteenth century and did not
hesitate to call the Negro slave trade 'a hateful commerce which makes
humanity shudder'.

Another reference to the controversy over the conquest of America
was made by the enlightened circles when Grégoire, formerly Bishop
of Blois and a member of the Institut de France, read before the
Faculty of Moral and Political Sciences, on 13 May 1801, a eulogy
of Las Casas. His purpose was to demonstrate the injustice of the
accusation levelled against Las Casas to the effect that it was he who
had instigated the introduction of Negro slaves into America.[1]

The discussion, in which Gregorio Funes, Dean of Córdoba de
Tucumán, Dr. Mier of Mexico, and Juan Antonio Llorente of Spain
later took part, is of little documentary value today; for all the prota-
gonists were unaware of the paragraph in the *Historia de las Indias*,
mentioned earlier in this paper, in which Las Casas explained that he
did, in fact, propose the introduction of Negroes to alleviate the bad
condition of the Indians, but later repented when he became aware of the
unjust methods used by the Portuguese in capturing and enslaving
Negroes, concluding that 'they have the same reasoning powers as the
Indians'.

A point that was clearly proved in this discussion at the beginning
of the nineteenth century was that Negro slaves had been taken to
Indo-America before Las Casas made his proposal.

But although this exchange of views is of minor interest from the point
of view of the subject under discussion, it is of the greatest value in
showing how the philosophers of the Enlightenment endorsed the
theories of Las Casas.

---

1. The documents are published in the *Colección de las Obras del Venerable Obispo de
Chiapa, Don Bartolomé de las Casas, defensor de la libertad de los Americanos*. Ed.
Juan Antonio Llorente, Paris, 1822, 2 vols., Vol. II, p. 329 et seq.

According to Bishop Grégoire, Las Casas was foremost among a number of generous-minded men who raised their voices against the oppressors and on behalf of the oppressed, vowing vengeance upon the former and invoking the protection of divine and human laws for the latter.

At the Congregation of Valladolid, in 1550, Sepúlveda maintained that it was fair to make war on the Indians in order to convert them to the faith. Las Casas refuted this argument, basing his contention on the principles of tolerance and freedom for all members of the human race; and those principles received the solemn approval of the Universities of Alcalá and Salamanca.

Grégoire considered it strange that, twenty years previously, the Madrid Academy of History should have published a magnificent edition of the works of that 'apologist for slavery' (Sepúlveda), whereas there was not yet one complete edition of the works of the 'virtuous' Las Casas. The Academy had not been ashamed to approve what it had itself called 'godly and just violence against pagans and heretics'. Grégoire hoped that the present members of the Academy were filled with loathing for 'so shocking a doctrine'.

In the Bishop's discourse there was no reference to the difference between natural and legal servitude, so much stressed in the sixteenth century. Sepúlveda was a thorough upholder of slavery and Las Casas a philanthropist defending the human race. Moreover, as he saw it, the controversy that had taken place in the sixteenth century was in fact only a prelude to the real battle in the eighteenth, and early nineteenth centuries—that is to say, the battle over Negro slavery. It was for this reason that Grégoire believed that Las Casas could not have been an advocate of the Negro slave trade and that such an imputation was slanderous: 'How could it have been possible for a man who, all his life, had claimed rights for all peoples regardless of colour, to become convinced that the black skin of those born in another hemisphere was a reason for condemning them to suffer cruel treatment by their masters? Men of character are consistent in their conduct. Their actions and principles are in unison. Accordingly, Benezet, Clarkson and the champions of the Negroes in general, far from accusing Las Casas, place him foremost among the defenders of mankind.' With the cause of the Indians thus linked with that of the Negroes, the campaign waged by Las Casas could be assimilated to that of the supporters of emancipation in the eighteenth century: 'Las Casas had many enemies; two centuries later he would have had many more'. His attitude towards the Spanish adventurers who enslaved Indians was comparable to that of the champions of the Negroes in France some years later towards the plantation owners: 'Have we not heard it said that the Negroes were a species somewhere between man and beast? In the same way the Spanish

59

colonists claimed that the Indians did not belong to the human race.'
Las Casas, enraged by the horrors he saw, pointed out the persons
responsible and roused the indignation of all sensitive minds.

Grégoire did not only see a formal affinity between the liberating
Christianity of the sixteenth century and the philanthropy of the
eighteenth, but he did establish a relationship between the respective
ideological content of the two centuries. He asserted that Las
Casas, a religious man like all benefactors of the human race, regarded
the people of all countries as members of a single family who ought
to love one another, to help one another and to enjoy the same rights.
He put into the mouth of Las Casas—the advocate of 'love towards all
men' and equality of rights—phrases appropriate to an enlightened
citizen at the time of the French revolution. For instance: what is of
import to all requires the consent of all; the curtailment of liberty is
inadmissible; the form of the political state should be determined by
the will of the people, for the people constitute the efficient cause of
government, and no charge can be imposed upon them without their
consent. Again, Las Casas is portrayed as maintaining that freedom is
the most precious of possessions and that, all nations being free, to wish
to bring them into subjection on the pretext that they are not Christian
is an offence against natural and Divine law; anyone who misuses his
authority is unworthy to exercise it, and no tyrant should be obeyed.
In defence of the Indians, the Spanish Friar is shown as invoking
natural law, which places all nations and individuals on an equal footing,
and Holy Scripture, which states that God is no respecter of persons;
by this means he threw into stronger relief the justice of the Indian claims.

Grégoire concluded by saying that, in the New World, a statue should
be put up in memory of Las Casas as a champion of human rights.
He knew no subject more worthy of engaging the talent of an admirer
of virtue, and it seemed to him strange that painting and poetry had
not yet turned their attention towards him. Those who prized religion,
morality, freedom and learning owed a tribute to the memory of one
whom Eguiara had called the 'ornament of America', and who, belonging
as he did to Spain by birth and to France by origin, might well be called
the 'ornament of the two worlds'. The Bishop added that the desire of
great men, who were almost always persecuted, was to exist in the future;
by reason of their talents, they were inevitably ahead of the thought
of their times, and they asked to be judged by posterity; and posterity,
heir to their virtue and talents, should pay the debt owed by their
contemporaries.

And so it was to be. When America had gained its independence,
Las Casas—'ahead of the thought of his times'—was honoured by
high-minded painters and poets and by sensitive people in general.
The new philosophy was attracted by 'Christian freedom' and, in order

to receive the heritage, first had to touch up the historical picture with some vigorous strokes of the brush. The differences were left in shadow and the resemblances were brought to the fore. But Grégoire was not an inventor. His discourse was reinforced by authentic passages from Las Casas. These provided grounds for the affinity he felt towards Las Casas and, on the other hand, for the repulsion he professed towards Sepúlveda, whose thought, though badly interpreted, was correctly appreciated intuitively with respect to its tendency to strengthen authority.

Some of the controversialists of the early nineteenth century, in order to reconcile their admiration for Las Casas with the fact, which they admitted, that he had supported the enslavement of Negroes, found it necessary to stress the existence of important differences between the thinking of the sixteenth century and that of the new age.

Funes pointed out to Bishop Grégoire that the possession of domestic slaves, acquired as the result of a just war, was permissible according to Las Casas' doctrine. In his century, the voice of philosophy and reason had not yet spoken with sufficient eloquence to induce, in this respect, the blessed revolution which it was to bring about later, whereby the inhuman practice of slavery was to be banished from the whole of Europe.

Mier observed that it was impossible to expect Las Casas, in the sixteenth century, to reason according to the ideas of the nineteenth. In Las Casas' time it never occurred to people to have scruples concerning the traffic in Negro slaves, and the whole of Christian Europe had until then engaged in that traffic with a perfectly easy conscience. 'Let us be quite clear on the subject; Christianity has recommended charity and meekness, and by teaching us that we are all sons of one Father and brothers in Jesus Christ, it gradually wears away the chains, lightens them; but one can be a good Christian and have slaves if they are legitimately acquired, treating them with Christian charity. Saint Paul, in order that the faithful (hearing that Jesus Christ has called us to freedom and brought us out of the servitude of sin and of the Mosaic Law) should not take this to mean corporal freedom, in his epistles constantly exhorts slaves to serve and obey their masters, like Christ himself. Philemon was a priest, and Saint Paul, although he had baptized his slave Onesimus and ordained him priest and had need of him for the apostolic ministry, did not reproach Philemon for being his master, but rather, because he was the master, sent the slave back to him, recommending Philemon to pardon him with the tenderness of a father. Under the laws of the Empire the acquisition of slaves was legitimate, and the Gospel does not run counter to civil laws.'

This speech serves as an apt reminder that Christian philosophy was not identical with the philosophy of the Enlightenment. Slavery was abolished because of a new trend of thought of which Mier approved; but, prior to this change, Christianity merely weakened, without breaking, the chains.

Llorente, like Funes, got over the distance between sixteenth-century Christianity and the philosophy of the Enlightenment by reference to the progress of ideas: 'Las Casas never wanted Negro slavery; but it existed and neither Las Casas nor anyone else thought it worth counting among the iniquitous acts of mankind, because the ideas then current in the whole of Europe concerning the Africans were entirely opposite to those we held nowadays when the concept of *jus gentium* is infinitely superior to what it was.'

Thus the apparently simple operation of 'bringing Las Casas forward in time' threw into relief the differences in the periods and ideas. Yet the affinity was irresistible; and the philosophers of the Enlightenment may well have been right to some extent in thinking that if Las Casas had lived 'two centuries later', he would have made common cause with them, both in demanding freedom for the Negroes and in championing the equalitarian political creed.

The Spanish and American echoes of this controversy resounded in the Cortes of Cádiz, but the Empire around which the ideas we have been considering revolved was already nearing its end.

The political doctrine that has been discussed in the foregoing pages fulfils an important function in the colonial history of America, for not only is it a part of the cultural legacy which has come down to us from the disco-verers, but it also serves as a means of uniting the two worlds without impairment of justice.

The dissemination of the idea of Christian freedom in the universities of Spanish-America, familiarity with the laws based upon that idea, and even the reflexion of the same liberal principle in the life of society, may be regarded as factors which helped to promote our own liberal convictions and to develop a sense of the brotherhood of mankind that stands in contrast to the 'defects' of natural servitude.

America thus possessed, from an early stage, a tradition of magnanimity that enabled her to resist the dangers of pride, prejudice and greed which also came in the wake of the first colonists.

Because they could draw upon the experience of these conflicts as precedents, American minds were more receptive, when the time came, to the philosophy of the Enlightenment, proclaiming equality between men and demanding new and better safeguards for individual freedom.

It is worth while stressing these precedents so as to correct the mistaken idea that we owe our independence and our liberalism solely to an ingenuous and chance imitation of foreign models suddenly put before the dazzled eyes of our forefathers.

Nowadays we realize that their aspirations (at the end of the eighteenth century and the beginning of the nineteenth) were in accord with a state of mind that had long existed—an enduring desire for justice and freedom which led them to venerate, among others, the fighting figure of Las Casas.

At that time, too, as during the Conquest, there was no lack of conflicting ideas and situations which had their roots in our earliest history. Therein lay the cause of another stubborn and tragic conflict.

The ideological conclusions that emerge from the present essay may be summed up as follows:

Freedom is an older attribute among us than has commonly been supposed.

Christianity brought to the New World ferments favourable to human freedom.

Those who have been defending the liberal conception of life since the time of the struggle for independence need not be ashamed of the past history of Spanish America in this respect, for it contains values capable of affording support and encouragement to that very defence.

It can be claimed, from what has been said in these pages, that the ideological history of America is inseparable from those universal aspirations in men's minds for the safeguard of human rights, the maintenance of order in the political community and the establishment of harmonious relations among peoples.

BIBLIOGRAPHY

ALTAMIRA, R. *Historia de España y de la civilización española*. Barcelona, 1906.

BELL, A. F. G. *Juan Ginés de Sepúlveda*. Oxford, 1925.

CARLYLE, R. W.; CARLYLE, A. J. *A history of mediaeval political theory in the West*, Edinburgh and London, 1930, 6 vols.

CARRANCÁ Y TRUJILLO, R. 'El estatuto jurídico de los esclavos en las postrimerías de la colonización española', *Revista de historia de América*, no. 3 (Mexico City, September 1938), p. 20-59.

EGUIARA Y EGUREN, J. J. de. *Prólogos a la biblioteca mexicana*. Version and study by A. Millares Carlo. Mexico City, 1944.

GERBI, A. *Viejas polémicas sobre el Nuevo Mundo*. 3rd ed., Lima, 1946.

GIMÉNEZ FERNÁNDEZ, M. *Instituciones jurídicas en la Iglesia Católica*. Madrid, 1940.

HANKE, L. *Las teorías políticas de Bartolomé de Las Casas*. Buenos Aires, 1935.

——. 'La controversia entre Las Casas y Sepúlveda', *Revista Universidad Católica Bolivariana*, Medellín, Colombia, 1942.

LAS CASAS, Bartolomé de. *Doctrina*, Prologue and selection by A. Yáñez. Mexico City, 1941.

MÉNDEZ PLANCARTE, G. *Humanistas del siglo XVIII*. Mexico City, 1941.

MENÉNDEZ PIDAL, R. *La España del Cid*. Madrid, 1929, 2 vols.

MILLARES CARLO, A. 'Feijóo en América', *Cuadernos Americanos*, 3rd year, vol. XV, no. 3 (May-June 1944) p. 139-60.

PARRY, J. H. *The Spanish theory of empire in the sixteenth century*. Cambridge, 1940.

PICÓN-SALAS, M. *De la conquista a la independencia. Tres siglos de historia cultural hispanoamericana*. Mexico City, 1944.

SEPÚLVEDA, J. G. de. *Tratado sobre las justas causas de la guerra contra los indios*. With a foreword by Marcelino Menéndez Pelayo and a study by Manuel García Pelayo. Mexico City, 1941.

TANNENBAUM, F. *Slave and citizen. The negro in the Americas*. New York, 1947.

WHITAKER, A. P. (ed.). *Latin America and the enlightenment*. New York, 1942.

ZAVALA, S. *Las instituciones jurídicas en la conquista de América*. Madrid, 1935.

——. *La encomienda indiana*. Madrid, 1935.

——. *Ensayos sobre la colonización española en América*. Buenos Aires, 1944.

——. *Servidumbre natural y libertad cristiana según los tratadistas españoles de los siglos XVI y XVII*. Buenos Aires, 1944.

——. *La filosofía política en la conquista de América*. Mexico City, 1947.